Which Election System is Best?

Stephen H. Sosnick

August 2014

Contents

Contents

Contents

Contents

List of Tables

List of Tables

Chapter 1

Introduction

An election system is a procedure for selecting one or more individuals for a specified status based on preferences expressed by members of a specified electorate. The status at issue usually is a executive office, such as governor, or one or more seats in a legislature, such as a city council.

To be eligible to win the office or seat, an individual (including a write-in candidate) usually must meet citizenship, residence, and age requirements and also must, within a specified period, file nominating documents and either pay a filing fee or present signatures from a specified number of people eligible to vote in the election.

The electorate, which often is called a "constituency", normally consists of individuals who, like the candidates, meet conditions pertaining to citizenship, residence, age, and registration. A geographic area containing lodgings that meet the residence requirement has various names, such as "election district", "electoral area", "trustee area", "ward", and "riding".

In the next two sections, we will review 22 different election systems. For each, we will describe how it chooses the winner(s), who uses the system, what tactics it leads voters to use, and its advantages and disadvantages. Especially when considering advantages and disadvantages, it will be helpful to divide the 22 election systems into two groups, namely, single-winner systems and multi-winner systems. This chapter identifies both the systems that will be discussed and the criteria that will be used in judging them.

1.1 Criteria for Evaluating Single-Winner Election Systems

A single-winner system is used when (a) an executive is being selected, (b) the specified electorate has merely one representative (as with U.S. congressional districts), or (c) although the electorate has two or more representatives, either their terms are staggered (as with U.S. senators) or one of the representatives has resigned or died.

We will consider twelve different single-winner systems. Each is either being used or being advocated. Their names are the column headings in Table 1.

Table 1 also lists ten criteria for evaluating a single-winner election system. Their names constitute the row headings in the table, and what each means is stated immediately below the table. The table has 120 blank cells, and we will fill them in Part 2.

1.2   Criteria for Evaluating Multi-Winner Election Systems

The single-winner election systems listed above are not the only way legislators are chosen. Often two or more representatives are chosen simultaneously in a multi-winner election. Some of the legislatures where that occurs are national and some are local, some have a single constituency and some have many, and some are unicameral while others are bicameral (in fact, about ⅓ of all national legislatures — and almost all of the national legislatures in countries with provincial legislatures as well as national and local legislatures — are bicameral). We will consider ten different multi-winner systems. Each is either being used or being advocated. Their names are the column headings in Table 2.

Table 2 also identifies eight criteria for evaluating a multi-winner election system. As in Table 1, the criteria constitute the row headings in the table, and the meaning of each criterion again is stated in a row beneath the table. The table has 80 blank cells, and we will fill them in in Part 3.

Table 1: Criteria for Evaluating the Single-Winner Election Systems Reviewed Below

	Simple Plurality	Runoff	Exhaustive	Full IRV	Coombs	Borda	Bucklin	Majority Judgment	Schulze	Maximin	Approval	Score
Elicits Ratings[1]	–	–	–	–	–	–	–	–	–	–	–	–
Condorcet Efficiency[2]	–	–	–	–	–	–	–	–	–	–	–	–
Mutual Majority[3]	–	–	–	–	–	–	–	–	–	–	–	–
Monotonic[4]	–	–	–	–	–	–	–	–	–	–	–	–
Later No Harm[5]	–	–	–	–	–	–	–	–	–	–	–	–
Independent of Clones[6]	–	–	–	–	–	–	–	–	–	–	–	–
Sincere Voting[7]	–	–	–	–	–	–	–	–	–	–	–	–
Transparent[8]	–	–	–	–	–	–	–	–	–	–	–	–
Vote Once[9]	–	–	–	–	–	–	–	–	–	–	–	–
Verifiable[10]	–	–	–	–	–	–	–	–	–	–	–	–

[1] Voters indicate the strength of their preferences.

[2] The probability that, when one of the candidates would receive more than half of the votes cast in a two-candidate runoff against each of the other candidates, that candidate will in fact be elected.

[3] If there is a subset of the candidates such that more than half of the voters strictly prefer every member of the subset to every candidate outside the subset, then the winner will come from the subset.

[4] Elevating the rank that a voter assigns to a particular candidate, while making no change in the order of other candidates, will not deprive that candidate of victory.

[5] Whether and how a voter ranks candidates below a particular candidate will not cause the latter candidate to lose the election.

[6] Suppose that two candidates are so alike that no voter would rank any other candidate between them. Then, if each of the two would be elected provided the other were not a candidate, one of the two will be elected if both are candidates. And, if each would lose provided the other were not a candidate, then each will lose if the other is a candidate.

[7] It is likely that voters will report their true preferences.

[8] It is easy for voters to understand how the outcome will be determined.

[9] The outcome will be determined with a single round of voting.

[10] The outcome can be confirmed simply by re-tallying ballots and re-adding subtotals.

Table 2: Criteria for Evaluating the Multi-Winner Election Systems Reviewed Below

	Multi-Winner Plurality	Limited Voting	Cumulative Voting	Single Transferable Vote	Multiple Transferable Vote	Constrained STV	Closed Lists	Open Lists	Parallel Voting	Mixed Member Proportional
Proportional[1]	–	–	–	–	–	–	–	–	–	–
Monotonic[2]	–	–	–	–	–	–	–	–	–	–
Voters Sovereign[3]	–	–	–	–	–	–	–	–	–	–
Automatic Allocation[4]	–	–	–	–	–	–	–	–	–	–
Independent of Clones[5]	–	–	–	–	–	–	–	–	–	–
Sincere Voting[6]	–	–	–	–	–	–	–	–	–	–
Transparent[7]	–	–	–	–	–	–	–	–	–	–
Verifiable[8]	–	–	–	–	–	–	–	–	–	–

[1] The proportion of open seats won by candidates favored by a faction of the voters and disfavored by other voters is as close to the proportion of votes cast by that faction as is possible, given that, when n seats are open, the fraction won must be $\frac{0}{n}$, $\frac{1}{n}$, $\frac{2}{n}$, ..., or $\frac{n}{n}$.

[2] Elevating the rank that a voter assigns to a particular candidate, while making no change in the order of other candidates, will not deprive that candidate of victory.

[3] Voters choose or rank individual candidates, not just lists of candidates.

[4] Votes are automatically apportioned among candidates as the voters casting those votes would wish if they knew which candidates needed additional support.

[5] Suppose that two candidates are so alike that no voter would rank any other candidate between them. Then, if each of the two would be elected provided the other were not a candidate, one of the two will be elected if both are candidates. And, if each would lose provided the other were not a candidate, then each will lose if the other is a candidate.

[6] It is likely that voters will report their true preferences.

[7] It is easy for voters to understand how the outcome will be determined.

[8] The outcome can be confirmed simply by re-tallying ballots and re-adding subtotals.

Part I

Twelve Single-Winner Election Systems

Chapter 2

How the Systems Differ

The single-winner systems discussed below differ in three respects. First, the systems differ in the number of times that the electorate votes in any one election. There are three different frequencies, as follows:

1. Ten of the systems ask voters to vote just once.

2. Another system asks voters to vote twice.

3. One system asks voters to vote until one candidate receives a decisive proportion of the votes cast.

Second, the systems elicit different information about voters' preferences. Four different ballots are used, as follows:

1. Three of the systems tell a voter to choose one candidate.

2. One system invites a voter to choose two or more candidates.

3. Six systems invite a voter to rank two or more candidates in order of preference.

4. Two system tell a voter to assign a rating — perhaps from 0 to 10 — to each candidate.

Third, the systems determine the winner differently. There are eight different rules, as follows:

1. One system awards the open seat to the leading vote getter.

2. Another system also awards the open seat to the leading vote getter, but only if the leader either receives more than, say, 40% of the votes cast or wins a runoff.

3. Three systems eliminate candidates one-by-one until one candidate receives more than, say, 50% of the votes cast.

4. Another system assigns a score to being ranked first on a ballot, a lower score to being ranked second, etc., and awards victory to the candidate with the largest total score.

5. Another system awards victory to the candidate who is ranked either first or second on the largest number of ballots.

6. Two systems see whether voters' rankings imply that one of the candidates would receive more than half of the votes cast in a two-candidate runoff regardless of which of the other candidates also was in that runoff and, if so, award victory to that candidate.

7. Another system awards the open seat to whichever candidate is approved by the largest number of voters.

8. Two systems award victory to whichever candidate has the highest average of voters' ratings.

Chapter 3

Illustrative Initial Conditions

To illustrate how each system works — and also to compare their outcomes — we will see which candidate each system would elect in a particular hypothetical case. In that case there are six candidates (namely, Abe, Ben, Cal, Dee, Eve, and Fay), three polling stations, and 27 voters, and the voters rank the candidates as indicated in Table 3. Here and below "Abe >Ben" means that the voter strictly prefers Abe to Ben.

Using this data, we will see that changing the election system changes the winner. Indeed, we will see that each of the six candidates wins with at least one of the election systems reviewed. That should make it clear that which system is used is important; it can affect which candidate wins.

Table 3: Rankings Used Below

	Ranking of Candidates	Number of Voters with that Ranking
Precinct 1	Abe >Ben >Dee >Eve >Cal >Fay	6
	Abe >Dee >Ben >Eve >Cal >Fay	1
	Abe >Fay >Dee >Cal >Ben >Eve	3
	Ben >Eve >Dee >Abe >Cal >Fay	1
	Ben >Fay >Eve >Dee >Cal >Abe	4
Precinct 2	Cal >Fay >Eve >Ben >Abe >Dee	1
	Cal >Fay >Eve >Dee >Ben >Abe	3
	Dee >Eve >Ben >Cal >Abe >Fay	1
	Dee >Eve >Fay >Ben >Abe >Cal	1
	Dee >Fay >Eve >Ben >Abe >Cal	1
Precinct 3	Eve >Fay >Cal >Ben >Abe >Dee	1
	Eve >Fay >Cal >Dee >Abe >Ben	1
	Eve >Fay >Cal >Dee >Ben >Abe	1
	Fay >Cal >Eve >Dee >Abe >Ben	1
	Fay >Dee >Eve >Cal >Abe >Ben	1
Total		27

Chapter 4

The Twelve Systems

4.1 Simple Plurality (also known as "Choose One", "Single-Winner Plurality", "Single-Member Plurality", "Single-Member Districts", "First Past the Post", and "The English system")

4.1.1 How the System Selects the Winner

An election is held to fill one opening. A voter may be offered a printed card for each official candidate and be told to put one of those cards in a ballot box. Alternatively, an official ballot may list individuals who are eligible to win the election and — perhaps leaving space for a write-in — tell a voter to choose one candidate.

For each valid ballot on which a qualified candidate is chosen, that candidate receives one "vote" (a vote is the unit of account in elections, analogous to the dollar in commerce). If one candidate receives more votes than any other candidate receives, then that candidate wins the election. If two or more candidates tie for most votes, then officials break the tie by lot.

4.1.2 Numerical Example

With the initial conditions shown in Table 3, six individuals, namely, Abe, Ben, Cal, Dee, Eve, and Fay, are eligible for a vacant seat and 27 persons are eligible to vote. If each eligible voter votes sincerely, then the ballots will show the choices listed in Table 4.

Because candidates receive one vote for each valid ballot on which they are chosen, Abe, Ben, Cal, Dee, Eve, and Fay initially receive, respectively, 10, 5, 4, 3, 3, and 2 votes. Since Abe received the most votes, Abe wins the election.

Table 4: Tally with Simple Plurality

	Candidate Chosen	Number of Voters Choosing that Candidate
Precinct 1	Abe	10
	Ben	5
Precinct 2	Cal	4
	Dee	3
Precinct 3	Eve	3
	Fay	2
	Total	27

4.1.3   Who Uses Simple Plurality

Many countries use simple plurality when electing their presidents. That occurs in Bosnia, Cameroon, Guinea, Guyana, Honduras, Iceland, Korea, Malawi, Mexico, Palestine, Panama, Paraguay, Philippines, Rwanda, Singapore, Taiwan, Tunisia, Venezuela, and Zambia. These countries also use simple plurality when electing governors, mayors, magistrates, and other public officials.[1]

In addition, part or all of many national legislatures consist of one representative per election district, elected by simple plurality. That occurs in Anguilla, Antigua, Bahamas, Bangladesh, Barbados, Belize, Bermuda, Botswana, Canada, Dominica, Ethiopia, Gambia, Ghana, Granada, India, Jamaica, Kenya, Malawi, Malaysia, Micronesia, Nepal, Nigeria, Oman, Palau, Saint Kitts, Saint Lucia, Saint Vincent, Solomons, Sudan, Swaziland, Tanzania, Trinidad, Turks & Caicos, Uganda, United Kingdom, United States, Yemen, Zambia, and Zimbabwe.

With single-member election districts, boundaries are very important. Under both U.S. and California rules, election districts, must be compact, (a) respect cities, counties, neighborhoods, and communities of interest, (b) enable minorities to elect and be elected, and (c) be of roughly equal population (some other countries equalize registration, not population). However, these objectives compete, so districting in the U.S. is subjective — and often serves the legislators who control it. In Canada, in contrast, a separate body draws the boundaries.

---

[1]This list of users — and similar lists included below — mostly come from Andrew Reynolds, Ben Reilly, and Andrew Ellis, Electoral System Design, International Institute for Democracy and Electoral Assistance, Stockholm, 2005, pp. 166–173.

Table 5a: Simple Plurality is not Condorcet Compliant — Preferences of Voters

Rankings of Candidates	Number of Voters with that Ranking
Abe >Ben >Cal	35
Ben >Cal >Abe	33
Cal >Ben >Abe	32
Total	100

4.1.4 Condorcet Compliance

A candidate may receive the most votes merely because two or more of the other candidates appeal to the same voters and spoil each other's chances. With simple plurality, therefore, one of those other candidates may lose despite being a "pairwise champion", that is, a candidate that would beat each of the other candidates in a head-to-head runoff. Tables 5a and 5b provides an illustration. Table 5b shows both the number of votes that the candidate in each row would receive in a pairwise election as well as their final results based on the rankings in Table 5a. For example, Ben would receive 30 votes in an election against Abe because 33 voters prefer Ben over all candidates, 32 prefer Ben over Abe but Cal over both of them and 35 prefer Abe over Ben. Note that even though Ben wins all of his paired comparisons against Abe and Cal, Abe wins the overall election.

Table 5b: Simple Plurality is not Condorcet Compliant — Paired Comparisons and Results

	Abe	Ben	Cal	Final Result of Election
Abe	–	$35 - 33 - 32 = -30$	$35 - 33 - 32 = -30$	35
Ben	$33 + 32 - 35 = 30$	–	$35 + 33 - 32 = 36$	33
Cal	$33 + 32 - 35 = 30$	$32 - 35 - 33 = -36$	–	32

According to French sociologist Maurice Duverger, practical politics tends to prevent that anomaly. "Duverger's Law" predicts that, in jurisdictions using simple plurality, two coalitions will emerge and that, by nominating just one candidate each for each office, the coalitions will avoid spoilers and vote-splitting.[2] In fact, however, both spoilers and

---

[2]See M. Duverger, "Duverger's Law: Forty Years Later," in B. Grofman and A. Lijphart, eds. Electoral Laws and Their Political Consequences, New York, Agathon Press, 1986.

vote-splitting do occur.

The concept of a pairwise champion — often called a "Condorcet alternative" — dates from 1785. In that year Nicolas de Condorcet, a French mathematician, proposed seeing whether there is a candidate that, if paired against each other candidate, one at a time, would in every case be preferred by more than half of the voters — and, if so, declaring that candidate the winner.[3] Condorcet pointed out that a candidate who is the first choice of a majority of the voters will be a pairwise champion, but a candidate may be a pairwise champion without being the first choice of a majority of the voters — for example, by being every voter's second choice.

In any one election, there may or may not be a Condorcet alternative. The likelihood drops if either the number of voters or the number of candidates rises. Simulations indicate that, when millions of people vote, the probability that one of the candidates will win all of his or her paired comparisons is about 91% with three candidates, falls to about 82% with four, falls to about 75% with five, and falls to about 68% with six. However, because the simulations assume that the probability that a voter ranks the candidates in a particular order is the same for every possible ordering (a worst-case assumption), these figures understate the actual probability that there is a pairwise champion.

4.1.5 Presidential Elections in the U.S.

A majority is required to elect the president of the United States, but the voters — an ad hoc group called the "Electoral College" — are chosen by simple plurality. Consequently, the president may be elected, not only having less than half of the popular vote, but even having fewer popular votes than the runner-up — as in fact occurred in 1824, 1876, 1888, and 2000.

In most states, electors' names do not appear on the ballot. Instead, the public votes for the real presidential candidates, and individuals pledged to a particular candidate, usually chosen at a party convention, become electors if that candidate receives the most votes. About half of the states have laws to punish electors who violate the pledge, and a few states also allow cancellation of a faithless vote.

In 1964, the number of electors became 538 — equal to one for each of the 435 congressional districts, plus 2 for each state, plus 3 from the District of Columbia. Maine since 1972 and Nebraska since 1992 in fact have chosen one elector in each congressional district, plus two electors statewide. In the other 48 states and D.C., one plurality-winner takes all of the jurisdiction's electors.

The Electoral College never meets. From the beginning (February 4, 1789), each state's electors have voted separately, usually in their state's capital. The votes are sealed and sent to the U.S. Senate for official tabulation. Since adoption of the 12th Amendment in

---

[3]Marie-Jean-Antoine-Nicolas de Caritat, Marquis de Condorcet. Essai sur l'Application de l'Analyse aux Probabilit's des Decisions prises ' la Pluralit' des Voix, Paris, 1785.

1804, each elector has cast one vote for president and one vote for vice president, and an absolute majority — currently 270 votes — is needed to elect.

If no candidate receives an absolute majority of the electors' votes, then Congress takes charge. The House of Representatives chooses one of whichever three candidates for president received the most votes from the Electoral College, and the Senate chooses one of whichever two candidates received the most votes for vice president. Each state's delegation casts one vote, and an absolute majority (now 26 votes) is still required to elect. Balloting continues until one candidate does receive a majority.

The House has chosen the president twice. It did so in 1801, when it chose Thomas Jefferson over Aaron Burr, and it did so in 1825, when it chose John Quincy Adams over Andrew Jackson and Henry Clay. Adams won immediately; Jefferson won after 36 ballots!

But 36 is not even a U.S. record. In 1924 the Democratic Party, meeting in Madison Square Garden in sweltering heat, chose John Davis as their candidate for president, but only when William McAdoo and Al Smith finally withdrew — after 100 ballots.

4.1.6   Tactical Voting with Simple Plurality

With simple plurality, a voting tactic called "compromising" (also known as "favorite betrayal") is quite common. It involves voting for a candidate who is not the voter's top choice in order to help that candidate defeat one or more other candidates.

For example, suppose that a chairman is to be elected, (a) Abe, Ben, and Cal are candidates, (b) simple plurality will be used to determine the winner, (c) nine voters will submit valid ballots, and (d) the preference ordering is (i) Abe >Ben >Cal for voters *1*, *2*, *3*, and *4*, (ii) Ben >Abe >Cal for voters *5*, *6*, and *7*, and (iii) Cal >Ben >Abe for voters *8* and *9*. Then, with sincere voting, Abe would receive 4 votes; Ben, 3; and Cal, 2. Hence, Abe would win, to the dismay of voters *8* and *9*.

However, suppose that voters *8* and *9*, anticipating that outcome, vote for Ben instead of Cal, while other voters vote sincerely. Then Abe would still receive 4 votes but Ben now would receive 5. Hence, the winner would change from Abe (the true third choice of voters *8* and *9*) to Ben (their true second choice).

Compromising is not wicked. Failure to compromise invites the "spoiler effect", that is, allows the candidacy of a non-winner to change the winner.

A famous example is the U.S. presidential race of 2000. In the electoral college, George W. Bush received 271 votes, Al Gore received 266, and there was one (faithless) abstention. In Florida, which gave Bush 25 electoral votes, Bush received just 537 more popular votes than Gore, while exit polls indicated that, if Ralph Nader, who received a total of 97,421 popular votes, had not run, 45% of Nader voters would have voted for Gore, 27% for Bush, and 28% for no one — and therefore Gore, not Bush, would have won. Since Nader did run, Nader supporters wanting to defeat Bush needed to compromise, but about 2,989 too few did so.

While compromising is not wicked, an election system that forces voters to choose between compromising and wasting their votes leaves something to be desired.

4.2 Runoff Voting (also known as "The 2-Round System", "The 2nd Ballot", and "The French System")

4.2.1 How the System Selects the Winner

An election is held to fill one opening. An official ballot lists individuals eligible to win the election, perhaps invites a write-in, and tells each voter to choose one candidate. Alternatively, a voter is offered a printed card for each candidate and puts one of the cards in a ballot box.

For each valid ballot on which a qualified candidate is chosen, that candidate receives one "vote", and whichever candidate receives the most votes wins the election, provided that candidate receives more than a specified proportion of the votes cast.

If no candidate receives more than the specified proportion, then a second round of voting occurs, and whichever of the finalists receives the most votes in that round wins the election. Officials break a tie, if one occurs, by lot.

Usually the finalists are whichever two candidates received the most votes in the first round. In that case, the election system is called "Top-2f." In elections for France's National Assembly, however, any candidate receiving at least 12.5% of the first round vote may enter the second round.

4.2.2 Numerical Example

With the initial conditions shown in Table 3, six individuals, namely, Abe, Ben, Cal, Dee, Eve, and Fay, are eligible for a vacant seat and 27 persons are eligible to vote. If each eligible voter votes sincerely, then the ballots will show the choices listed in Table 6a.

Because candidates initially receive one vote for each valid ballot on which they are chosen, Abe, Ben, Cal, Dee, Eve, and Fay initially receive, respectively, 10, 5, 4, 3, 3, and 2 votes, a total of 27 votes. Assume that the rules say that the leading vote-getter wins without a runoff if — and only if — he or she receives more than 40% of the votes cast; otherwise, there is a runoff between the two leading vote-getters. Here, 40% is 10.8, so none of the candidates wins on the initial tally.

Abe and Ben are the front-runners, so officials next invite voters to choose between them. Given the same voters, the rankings we have assumed, and sincere voting, the runoff ballots will show the choices listed in Table 6b.

So, with runoff voting, candidate Ben wins, 14 votes to 13. With simple plurality, in contrast, Abe would have won (see above).

Table 6a: Initial Tally with Runoff Voting

	Candidate Chosen	Number of Voters Choosing that Candidate
Precinct 1	Abe	10
	Ben	5
Precinct 2	Cal	4
	Dee	3
Precinct 3	Eve	3
	Fay	2
	Total	27

Table 6b: Second Tally with Runoff Voting

	Candidate Chosen	Number of Voters Choosing that Candidate
Precinct 1	Abe	10
	Ben	5
Precinct 2	Cal	4
	Dee	3
Precinct 3	Eve	3
	Fay	2
	Total	27

4.2.3 Who Uses Runoff Voting

A majority of countries with an elected president use runoff voting — in particular, Top-2 — when electing their president. That occurs in Afghanistan, Algeria, Angola, Argentina, Armenia, Austria, Azerbaijan, Belarus, Benin, Bolivia, Brazil, Bulgaria, Burkina Faso, Cape Verde, Central African Republic, Chad, Chile, Colombia, Congo Brazzaville, Costa Rica, Cote D'Ivoire, Croatia, Cyprus, Czech Republic, Djibouti, Dominican Republic, Ecuador, Egypt, El Salvador, Finland, France, Gabon, Gambia, Georgia, Ghana, Guatemala, Guinea-Conakry, Guinea-Bissau, Haiti, Indonesia, Iran, Kazakhstan, Kenya, Kyrgyzstan, Lithuania, Macedonia, Madagascar, Mali, Mauritania, Mongolia, Mozambique, Namibia, Nicaragua, Niger, Nigeria, Palau, Peru, Poland, Portugal, Romania, Russia, Sao Tome, Senegal, Seychelles, Sierra Leone, Slovakia, Slovenia, Sudan, Tajikistan, Tanzania, Timor-Leste, Togo, Turkmenistan, Uganda, Ukraine, Uruguay, Uzbekistan, Yemen, and Zimbabwe.

In Chile, the runoff occurs four weeks after the initial vote, but in France — and, most often, in other countries too — the runoff occurs just two weeks after.

What triggers a runoff for president varies from country to country. In Nicaragua, a runoff occurs unless the front-runner receives at least 35% of the vote and at least five points more than the runner-up. In Costa Rica, the front-runner needs at least 40% of the vote. In Argentina, a runoff occurs unless the front-runner receives either at least 45% of the vote or at least 40% and a 10-point lead. In Bolivia, a runoff occurs unless the front-runner receives either more than 50% of the vote or at least 40% and a 10-point lead. In Brazil, Bulgaria, France, Poland, Senegal, and Slovenia, a runoff occurs unless the front-runner receives more than 50%. In Indonesia, a runoff occurs unless the front-runner receives both more than 50% overall and more than 20% in at least half of the provinces. In Nigeria, a runoff occurs unless the front-runner receives both more than 50% overall and more than 25% in at least ⅔ of the federal states. In Sierra Leone, a runoff occurs unless the front-runner receives at least 55%. So the threshold varies; to avoid a second round of voting, 35%–55%, and maybe some breadth, is needed.

Various countries also use runoff voting, together with election districts, having a single representative, when electing part or all of the national legislature. That occurs in Bahrain, Belarus, Central African Republic, Comoros, Congo Brazzaville, Cuba, Egypt, France, Gabon, Haiti, Iran, Kiribati, North Korea, Kyrgyzstan, Mali, Mauritania, Mongolia, Montserrat, Togo, Turkmenistan, Uzbekistan, and Vietnam.

For France's National Assembly, the runoff occurs merely one week after the initial poll.

Top-2 is popular in the U.S. California has used it for all congressional and state-government elections (except Superintendent of Public Instruction) since 2012, with no write-ins in the runoff and (uniquely) a runoff occurring even if there were only two candidates initially. Washington State also uses Top-2, and Georgia and Louisiana have runoffs in congressional races if no candidate tops 50%. Burlington, VT, after twice using instant-runoff voting to elect its mayor, returned to Top-2 in 2010 (a runoff occurring unless the leading vote-getter receives more than 40%).

Federal law requires states to hold congressional elections in November and also requires that registrars mail ballots to overseas and military voters at least 45 days before a federal election — though, in practice, about 70 days are needed before a runoff can be held. California, however, holds its primary election in June, so the runoffs occur about five months — 150 days! — later.

4.2.4 Condorcet Efficiency of Runoff Voting

Two candidates may reach the runoff merely because other candidates appealed to the same voters and spoiled each other's chances. Evidently this occurred in Egypt in May 2012, when Mohammed Morsi and Ahmed Shafiq, with 24% and 23% of the total vote for president, respectively, made the runoff, while candidates supported by the rebels of Tahrir Square were eliminated despite collectively receiving a majority of the total vote. Hence, runoff voting, like simple plurality, does not guarantee that, when there is a Condorcet alternative, that is, a candidate that would win a runoff against each of the other candidates, that candidate will in fact win the election.

But runoff voting is much less likely to fail than simple plurality. A simulation by Samuel Merrill indicated that, with 25 voters, runoff voting will raise the conditional probability that a Condorcet alternative will win, given that one exists, from 0.79 to 0.96 with three candidates, from 0.69 to 0.90 with four candidates, from 0.62 to 0.84 with five candidates, from 0.52 to 0.74 with seven candidates, and from 0.43 to 0.61 with ten candidates. These increases are impressive.

The spoiler effect also is noteworthy. Because nominating a loser can affect both whether there is a runoff and which candidates enter the runoff, runoff voting is vulnerable to the spoiler effect, that is, to allowing nomination of a candidate who does not win to change the winner.

However, runoff voting is less vulnerable than simple plurality to the spoiler effect. To see why, suppose that a candidate runs who does not come in first or second but who does divert enough votes from another candidate to drop that other candidate from first place to second and raise the candidate who would have been second to first. That will change the outcome with simple plurality but presumably will not change the outcome with runoff voting.

4.2.5 Tactics with Runoff Voting

Runoff voting, like simple plurality, can reward compromising, that is, voting for a candidate who is not the voter's top choice in order to help that candidate defeat one or more other candidates.

Compromising can be useful if the initial tally affects either whether a runoff occurs or which candidates enter the runoff.

For example, suppose that (a) a mayor is to be elected, (b) Abe, Ben, and Cal are candidates, (c) runoff voting will determine the winner, (d) there will be runoff unless the front-runner receives more than 50% on the initial tally, (e) nine voters will submit valid ballots, and (f) the preference ordering is (i) Abe >Cal >Ben for voters *1*, *2*, *3*, and *4*, (ii) Ben >Abe >Cal for voters *5*, *6*, and *7*, and (iii) Cal >Ben >Abe for voters *8* and *9*.

Then, with sincere voting, votes received on the first tally would be 4 for Abe, 3 for Ben, and 2 for Cal. Hence, Cal would be eliminated. On the second tally, votes would be 4 for Abe and 5 for Ben, and therefore Ben would be elected, to the dismay of voters *1*, *2*, *3*, and *4*.

However, suppose that voters *1* and *2*, anticipating that outcome, choose Cal (their second choice) instead of Abe, while other voters vote sincerely. Then votes received on the first tally would be $4 - 2 = 2$ for Abe, 3 for Ben, and $2 + 2 = 4$ for Cal. Hence, Abe would be eliminated. On the second tally, votes received would be $4 + 2 = 6$ for Cal and 3 for Ben. Hence, the winner would change from Ben (the actual third choice of voters *1* and *2*) to Cal (their actual second choice).

Runoff voting also can reward compromising if, as in elections to France's National Assembly, more than two candidates can enter the runoff. A second round with three or more candidates is, in effect, a Simple Plurality election.

On the other hand, compromising is less likely to be helpful — and therefore is less likely — with the Top-2 version of Runoff than with simple plurality. With Top-2, a voter favoring a minor candidate can vote sincerely in the initial round, anticipating that his vote will not affect either whether there is a runoff or which two candidates are in the runoff, and then again vote sincerely for whichever of this two finalists he prefers.

4.3 Exhaustive Voting and Repeated Voting

4.3.1 How the System Selects the Winner

An election is held to fill one opening. An official ballot lists individuals eligible to win the election, perhaps invites a write-in, and tells voters to choose one candidate — or, in some cases, to vote "Yes" or "No" for the current nominee (e.g., for prime minister). Alternatively, a voter receives a printed card for each official candidate and puts one of the cards in the ballot box.

For each valid ballot on which a qualified candidate is chosen, the candidate receives one "vote." If one of the candidates receives more than a required proportion of the votes cast — usually, half — then that candidate wins the election. If two candidates receive exactly half of the votes cast, then the winner is determined by chance.

If no candidate wins on the initial tally, then, with Exhaustive Voting, the candidate receiving the fewest votes is eliminated (a tie, if one occurs, being broken by lot), and a second ballot tells voters to choose one of the remaining candidates. With Repeated

Voting, in contrast, individual candidates decide when to withdraw, so the next ballot offers voters the same alternatives until a withdrawal in fact occurs.[4]

Re-voting and re-counting continue until one of the candidates either (a) has more than the required proportion of the votes cast, or (b) has exactly half of the votes cast and wins a tie-break with another candidate who also has exactly half. That candidate wins the election.

4.3.2 Numerical Example of Exhaustive Voting

With initial conditions shown in Table 3, six individuals, namely, Abe, Ben, Cal, Dee, Eve, and Fay, are eligible for a vacant seat and 27 persons are eligible to vote. If each eligible voter votes sincerely, then the ballots (identified now by faction instead of by precinct) will show the choices listed in Table 7a.

Table 7a: Initial Tally with Exhaustive Voting

	Candidate Chosen	Number of Voters Choosing that Candidate
Faction 1	Abe	10
	Ben	5
Faction 2	Cal	4
	Dee	3
Faction 3	Eve	3
	Fay	2
	Total	27

Each of the candidates received less than half of the votes cast (Abe, the front-runner, has merely 10 of the 27 votes). Fay, with 2 votes, received the fewest. Hence, Fay is eliminated, and officials ask voters to choose one of the five other candidates. Given the same voters, the rankings we have assumed, and sincere voting, the ballots will now show the choices listed in Table 7b.

Again each of the candidates received less than half of the votes cast (Abe, the front-runner, still has merely 10 of the 27 votes). Eve, with three votes, received the fewest.

---

[4]Along with much else, Duncan Black gave us the name "Exhaustive Voting" in The Theory of Committees and Elections, Cambridge University Press, 1958; see p. 69. Who gave us the name "Repeated Voting" is unknown.

Table 7b: Second Tally with Exhaustive Voting

	Candidate Chosen	Number of Voters Choosing that Candidate
Faction 1	Abe	10
	Ben	5
Faction 2	Cal	4
	Dee	3
Faction 3	Eve	3
	Cal	1
	Dee	1
	Total	27

Hence, Eve is eliminated and voters are invited to choose one of the four remaining candidates. Given the same voters, the rankings we have assumed, and sincere voting, the ballots will now show the choices listed in Table 7c.

Again each of the candidates received less than half of the votes cast (Abe, the front-runner, still has merely 10 of the 27 votes). Now Dee, with four votes, received the fewest. Consequently, Dee is eliminated and voters are invited to choose one of the three remaining candidates. Given the same voters, the rankings we have assumed, and sincere voting, the ballots will now show the choices listed in Table 7d.

Again each of the candidates received less than half of the votes cast (Abe, the front-runner, still has merely 10 of the 27 votes). Ben, with 8 votes, received the fewest. Hence, Ben is eliminated and voters are invited to choose one of the two remaining candidates. Given the same voters, the rankings we have assumed, and sincere voting, the ballots will now show the choices listed in Table 7e.

At last, one of the candidates has more than half of the votes cast. That is Cal, who has 14 of the 27 votes cast and therefore wins the election. In contrast, as seen above, the winner would have been Abe with Simple Plurality and Ben with Runoff Voting.

4.3.3   Who Uses Exhaustive and Repeated Voting

Many selections are made by Exhaustive or Repeated Voting. Exhaustive Voting is used when the International Olympic Committee and the FIFA World Cup choose a host city. Repeated Voting is used to choose the president of the European Parliament, the speaker of the House of Commons in Britain and Canada, and members of the Swiss Federal Council.

Table 7c: Third Tally with Exhaustive Voting

	Candidate Chosen	Number of Voters Choosing that Candidate
Faction 1	Abe	10
	Ben	5
Faction 2	Cal	4
	Dee	3
Faction 3	Cal	3
	Cal	1
	Cal	1
	Total	27

Table 7d: Fourth Tally with Exhaustive Voting

	Candidate Chosen	Number of Voters Choosing that Candidate
Faction 1	Abe	10
	Ben	5
Faction 2	Cal	4
	Ben	3
Faction 3	Cal	3
	Cal	1
	Cal	1
	Total	27

Table 7e: Fifth Tally with Exhaustive Voting

	Candidate Chosen	Number of Voters Choosing that Candidate
Faction 1	Abe	10
	Abe	1
	Cal	4
Faction 2	Cal	4
	Cal	1
	Abe	2
Faction 3	Cal	3
	Cal	1
	Cal	1
	Total	27

Repeated Voting also is used when a city council chooses a mayor and when a parliament or political party chooses a prime minister.

4.3.4   Condorcet Efficiency of Exhaustive Voting

Exhaustive Voting and Repeated Voting, like runoff voting, do not guarantee that, if one of the candidates is a Condorcet alternative (that is, a pairwise champion), then that candidate will win the election. But, if one of the candidates in fact is a Condorcet alternative, then that candidate is more likely to win with Exhaustive Voting or Repeated Voting than with runoff voting. Merrill's simulation indicates that, with 25 voters, using Exhaustive Voting instead of runoff voting will raise the conditional probability that a Condorcet alternative will win, given that one exists, from 0.90 to 0.93 with four candidates, from 0.84 to 0.89 with five candidates, from 0.74 to 0.85 with seven candidates, and from 0.61 to 0.78 with ten candidates.[5] Impressive increases!

4.3.5   Presidential Elections in Germany

Repeated voting, limited to three rounds, is used in electing the president of Germany (a mostly-ceremonial office with a five-year term). The electorate, called the "Federal Convention", consists of all (622 in 2012) members of the Bundestag (the "lower" house of

---

[5]Samuel Merrill, Am. J. Pol. Sci., 28:23–48, 1984.

the national legislature), plus an equal number of politicians or celebrities chosen by the 16 Länder (states). Additional candidates may be nominated after either the first or second round of voting, and the winner is whichever candidate receives an absolute majority (623 or more votes in 2012) in the first or second round or receives the most votes in a third round. In fact, it took three rounds to elect Christian Wulff in 2010, but — because the leading parties concurred — only one round to elect Joachim Gauck in an early election in 2012.

4.3.6 Election of the Roman Catholic Pope

The Papal Conclave uses a version of Repeated Voting. It did so most recently when 115 cardinals convened in the Sistine Chapel in March 2013. At each round, each voter writes a name on a piece of paper and puts it in an urn. Voting continues, up to four times per day, until one candidate receives more than ⅔ of the votes (a rule written by the Lateran Council of 1179). However, after 33 rounds, votes are counted only for whichever two individuals received the most votes in the previous round.

4.3.7 Election of the Coptic Pope

Repeated voting with a random element is used in selecting the leader of the Coptic Orthodox Church of Alexandria (the largest Christian group in the Arab world), most recently in November 2012. A committee identified five candidates, and 2,400 members of the church's Holy Synod and General Lay Council narrowed the field to three. Then, in St. Mark Cathedral in Cairo, a blindfolded boy drew one of three folded pieces of paper from a transparent chalice. The name on that piece of paper — and therefore the new pope — was Bishop Tawadros of El Beheira.

4.4 Instant-Runoff Voting (also known as "IRV", "The Alternative Vote", "The Hare System", and "Ranked-Choice Voting")

4.4.1 How the System Selects the Winner

An election is held to fill one position. An official ballot lists individuals eligible to win the election, perhaps invites a write-in, and invites each voter to rank the candidates in order of preference.

In some places (e.g., Australia) voters rank candidates by writing "1" in the box next to their first choice, "2" in the box next to their second choice, etc., and operators data-punch the numbers for processing.

Elsewhere (e.g., in Scotland and Portland, ME) voters use a Marksense card to rank candidates, marking one oval in the first-choice column of ovals, marking another oval in the second-choice column, etc. The marked ballots can be optically scanned, and voters' rankings can be processed either manually or by computer.

Qualified candidates initially receive one "vote" for each ballot on which they are first choice, and a candidate wins on the initial tally either (a) by receiving more than half of the votes tallied, or (b) by receiving exactly half and then winning a tie-break with another candidate who also received exactly half.

If no candidate wins on the initial tally, then officials identify the candidate who received the fewest votes on the first tally (breaking a tie, if one occurred, randomly) and eliminate that candidate from contention.

Eliminating the straggler may cause two kinds of adjustment.

First, any ballot on which only the eliminated candidate is ranked is thereafter treated as if it never existed. That reduces the number of votes needed for election in a subsequent tally.

Second, on any ballot where other candidates are ranked and the eliminated candidate is ranked above at least one of them, each lower-ranked candidate advances one rank — for example, advances from second to first.

Who makes these adjustments? That depends on whether the polling stations (a) send voters' ballots (or images thereof) to election headquarters for processing (something easily done in municipal elections), or (b) tally and report first choices and then wait for instructions (as often would occur in California, where ballots are processed in county election offices). In either case, the process is controlled centrally.

After the adjustments are made, officials make a second count of voters' top choices. As on the initial tally, a candidate wins either (a) by receiving more than half of the votes currently tallied, or (b) by receiving exactly half and then winning a tie-break with another candidate who also received exactly half. If there is still no winner, officials continue eliminating, making the two adjustments, and recounting until one of the candidates does either have more than half of the current vote-total or wins a tie-break with another candidate who also has exactly half.

4.4.2 Numerical Example

With the raw data in Table 3, six individuals, namely, Abe, Ben, Cal, Dee, Eve, and Fay, are eligible for a vacant seat and 27 persons are eligible to vote. If each eligible voter votes sincerely, then the ballots will show the rankings listed in Table 8a.

Tallying those 27 ballots gives Abe, Ben, Cal, Dee, Eve, and Fay, respectively, 10, 5, 4, 3, 3, and 2 votes.

Each of the candidates received fewer than half of the total of 27 votes, so no candidate wins on the initial tally.

Fay received the fewest votes on that tally, so Fay will be eliminated.

(Officials could simultaneously eliminate both Fay and the candidate with the next fewest votes if the sum of the votes for Fay and for that candidate were less than the votes

Table 8a: Initial Tally with Instant-Runoff Voting

	Rank Assigned to Candidate:						Number of Voters Assigning Those Ranks
	Abe	Ben	Cal	Dee	Eve	Fay	
	1	2	5	3	4	6	6
	1	3	5	2	4	6	1
Precinct 1	1	5	4	3	6	2	3
	4	1	5	3	2	6	1
	6	1	5	4	3	2	4
	5	4	1	6	3	2	1
	6	5	1	4	3	2	3
Precinct 2	5	3	4	1	2	6	1
	5	4	6	1	2	3	1
	5	4	6	1	3	2	1
	5	4	3	6	1	2	1
	5	6	3	4	1	2	1
Precinct 3	6	5	3	4	1	2	1
	5	6	2	4	3	1	1
	5	6	4	2	3	1	1
						Total	27

for the candidate with the next fewest votes after that — but that is not the case here.)

There is no ballot on which only Fay is ranked, so all 27 ballots are still relevant; none is "exhausted".

On 9 of the 27 ballots, Fay is ranked last (that is, Fay is either sixth or unranked). Fay's elimination has no effect on these ballots other than, in effect, to erase Fay.

On 18 other ballots, Fay is ranked above at least one other candidate. On these 18 ballots, each of the lower-ranked candidates now moves up one rank.

With Fay eliminated and ranks adjusted accordingly, the ballots have the rankings shown in Table 8b.

Table 8b: Second Tally with Instant-Runoff Voting

	Rank Assigned to Candidate:						Number of Voters Assigning Those Ranks
	Abe	Ben	Cal	Dee	Eve	~~Fay~~	
	1	2	5	3	4	–	6
	1	3	5	2	4	–	1
Precinct 1	1	4	3	2	5	–	3
	4	1	5	3	2	–	1
	5	1	4	3	2	–	4
	4	3	1	5	2	–	1
	5	4	1	3	2	–	3
Precinct 2	5	3	4	1	2	–	1
	4	3	5	1	2	–	1
	4	3	5	1	2	–	1
	4	3	2	5	1	–	1
	4	5	2	3	1	–	1
Precinct 3	5	4	2	3	1	–	1
	4	5	1	3	2	–	1
	4	5	3	1	2	–	1
						Total	27

Candidates again receive one vote for each ballot on which they are now first choice, so Abe, Ben, Cal, Dee, and Eve now have 10, 5, 5, 4, and 3 votes, respectively, and the total is still 27 votes.

Again each of the candidates has less than half of the votes cast.

Eve, with three votes, has the fewest. Hence, Eve is now eliminated.

There is no ballot on which only Eve is ranked, so all 27 ballots are still relevant; none is ignored.

On three ballots of the 27 ballots, Eve is ranked last (that is, is either fifth or unranked). Eve's elimination has no effect on other ranks on these ballots.

On 24 other ballots, Eve is ranked above at least one candidate whose rank can be elevated. On these 24 ballots, each of the lower-ranked candidates now moves up one rank.

With Eve eliminated and ranks adjusted accordingly, the ballots have the rankings shown in Table 8c.

Table 8c: Third Tally with Instant-Runoff Voting

| | Rank Assigned to Candidate: | | | | | | Number of Voters Assigning Those Ranks |
	Abe	Ben	Cal	Dee	~~Eve~~	~~Fay~~	
	1	2	4	3	–	–	6
	1	3	4	2	–	–	1
Precinct 1	1	4	3	2	–	–	3
	3	1	4	2	–	–	1
	4	1	3	2	–	–	4
	3	2	1	4	–	–	1
	4	3	1	2	–	–	3
Precinct 2	4	2	3	1	–	–	1
	3	2	4	1	–	–	1
	3	2	4	1	–	–	1
	3	2	1	4	–	–	1
	3	4	1	2	–	–	1
Precinct 3	4	3	1	2	–	–	1
	3	4	1	2	–	–	1
	3	4	2	1	–	–	1
						Total	27

Abe, Ben, Cal, and Dee now have 10, 5, 8, and 4 votes, respectively, and the total is still 27.

Again each of the candidates has less than half of the votes cast. Dee, with four votes, has the fewest. Hence, Dee is now eliminated.

There is no ballot on which only Dee is ranked, so all 27 ballots are still relevant; none is ignored.

On 2 ballots Dee is ranked last (that is, is either fourth or unranked). Dee's elimination has no effect on other ranks on these ballots.

On 25 other ballots, Dee is ranked above at least one candidate whose rank can be elevated. On these 25 ballots, each of the lower-ranked candidates now moves up one rank.

With Dee eliminated and ranks adjusted accordingly, the ballots have the rankings shown in Table 8d.

Table 8d: Fourth Tally with Instant-Runoff Voting

	Rank Assigned to Candidate:						Number of Voters Assigning Those Ranks
	Abe	Ben	Cal	~~Dee~~	~~Eve~~	~~Fay~~	
	1	2	3	–	–	–	6
	1	2	3	–	–	–	1
Precinct 1	1	3	2	–	–	–	3
	2	1	3	–	–	–	1
	3	1	2	–	–	–	4
	3	2	1	–	–	–	1
	3	2	1	–	–	–	3
Precinct 2	3	1	2	–	–	–	1
	2	1	3	–	–	–	1
	2	1	3	–	–	–	1
	3	2	1	–	–	–	1
	2	3	1	–	–	–	1
Precinct 3	3	2	1	–	–	–	1
	2	3	1	–	–	–	1
	2	3	1	–	–	–	1
						Total	27

Abe, Ben, and Cal now have 10, 8, and 9 votes, respectively, and the total is still 27. Again each of the candidates has less than half of the votes cast. Ben, with 8 votes, has the fewest. Hence, Ben is now eliminated.

There is no ballot on which only Ben is ranked, so all 27 ballots are still relevant; none is ignored.

On six ballots Ben is ranked last (that is, is either third or unranked). Ben's elimination has no effect on other ranks on these ballots.

On 21 other ballots, Ben is ranked above at least one candidate whose rank can be elevated. On these 21 ballots, each of the lower-ranked candidates now moves up one rank.

With Ben eliminated and ranks adjusted accordingly, the ballots have the rankings shown in Table 8e.

Table 8e: Fifth Tally with Instant-Runoff Voting

		Rank Assigned to Candidate:					Number of Voters Assigning Those Ranks
	Abe	~~Ben~~	Cal	~~Dee~~	~~Eve~~	~~Fay~~	
	1	–	2	–	–	–	6
	1	–	2	–	–	–	1
Precinct 1	1	–	2	–	–	–	3
	1	–	2	–	–	–	1
	2	–	1	–	–	–	4
	2	–	1	–	–	–	1
	2	–	1	–	–	–	3
Precinct 2	2	–	1	–	–	–	1
	1	–	2	–	–	–	1
	1	–	2	–	–	–	1
	2	–	1	–	–	–	1
	2	–	1	–	–	–	1
Precinct 3	2	–	1	–	–	–	1
	2	–	1	–	–	–	1
	2	–	1	–	–	–	1
						Total	27

Abe and Cal now have 13 and 14 votes, respectively, and the total is still 27. So at last — on the fifth tally — one of the candidates has more than half of the votes cast. That is candidate Cal, who therefore wins the election.

It is not a coincidence that the winner with IRV, that is, Cal, is the same as with Exhaustive Voting. IRV produces the same result as Exhaustive Voting without requiring that voters assemble in one place or register their preferences more than once.

It is also no accident that the winner in earlier sections was different — namely, Abe with Simple Plurality and Ben with Runoff Voting. Our numerical examples are designed to show that changing the election system, except between IRV and Exhaustive Voting, can change the winner even though voters' preferences do not change.

4.4.3 Who Uses IRV

American architect William Ware devised IRV in 1871, but its first public use was in Australia in 1893. From there, IRV spread around the world.

The Republic of Ireland uses IRV to elect its president (a mostly-ceremonial position with a seven-year term). Several dozen counting centers, scattered around the country, report their current counts to a central office. In turn, the central office sends instructions about which candidate to eliminate from the next tally.

Australia uses IRV, together with single-member election districts, to elect all representatives in both the national House of Representatives and the "lower" houses of five of the six Australian states. By phone on election night, polling stations report their count of first choices to a Division Officer who, in turn, enters the data into a computerized system. The system processes the data and posts the results on a website.

Following Australia's lead, both Fiji (which gained independence from Britain in 1970) and Papua New Guinea (which gained independence from Australia in 1975) use IRV to elect their parliaments — which, however, are unicameral.

Nine U.S. cities are using IRV, as follows: San Francisco, CA (mayor, supervisors, and school board since 2004); Takoma Park, MD (mayor, city council, and school board since 2006); Minneapolis, MN (mayor, city council, and school board since 2009); Oakland, CA, Berkeley, CA, and San Leandro, CA (mayor, city council, and school board since 2010); and St. Paul, MN, Portland, ME, and Telluride, CO (mayor and city council since 2011). In addition, Hendersonville, NC and Memphis, TN will start when equipment arrives that can scan ballots, prepare multi-precinct tallies, redistribute votes as candidates are eliminated, and be publicly audited and verified.

IRV also is used to elect (a) some city mayors in the United Kingdom and New Zealand, (b) the leaders of Canada's Liberal Party and of the UK's Labour Party and Liberal Democrats; (c) officers of the American Chemical Society, American Psychological Association, American Psychiatric Association, American Association of University Women, and American Mensa, (d) the Best Picture of the Academy of Motion Pictures; and (e) about 55 student governments in the United States, including University of California, Davis, University of California, Berkeley, UCLA, Stanford, Cal Tech, MIT, Columbia, Cornell, Duke, and Harvard.

On the other hand, some jurisdictions have tried IRV and rejected it. After one or two uses, IRV was discontinued in Ann Arbor MI in 1976 and in Aspen CO, Tacoma, WA, and Burlington, VT in 2009–2010.

In addition, voters in some places have rejected IRV without trying it. That occurred in Cincinnati, OH in 1988, 1991, and 2008, in British Columbia in 2009, and both in Fort Collins, CO and for the Parliament of the United Kingdom in 2011. Opponents cited extra costs, voter confusion, long lines, and delay from absentee and provisional ballots.

Incidentally, Californians for Electoral Reform (CfER, pronounced SEE-fur), a public-interest group founded in 1993, brought IRV to the Bay Area. In 1996, the organization led a campaign to bring a multi-winner version of IRV to San Francisco. When the campaign failed, CfER decided to focus on IRV, and it succeeded in bringing IRV first to San Francisco and then to Berkeley, CA, Oakland, CA, and San Leandro, CA.

4.4.4 Presidential Elections in India

India uses a version of instant-runoff voting to elect its president (a mostly-ceremonial office with a five-year term). The electorate consists of the elected members of both houses of the national legislature (Lok Sabha and Rajya Sabha), each member having a vote currently valued at 708, and also of the elected members of the legislative assemblies of the states and territories, each having a vote whose value depends on the population represented (for example, the value of a vote for an MLA from Uttar Pradesh is 208 and for an MLA from Sikkim is 7). To win, a candidate must receive more than 50% of the total value of votes cast, and — until one does have a majority — candidates are eliminated one by one and votes for them are transferred to the voters' next choices.

4.4.5 Merits and Demerits of IRV

Instant-Runoff Voting has some noteworthy advantages. Unlike runoff voting, IRV avoids the delay, public and private expense, and turnover of voters associated with re-voting — and, unlike Exhaustive Voting, avoids turnover without requiring that the electorate assemble in one place.

Also, because candidates hoping that voters who favor someone else will at least rank them second, IRV discourages negative campaigning against candidates who are likely to be eliminated before the final tally, that is, candidates other than a front-runner.

Moreover, IRV encourages sincere voting. Unless a voter can anticipate the order in which candidates will be eliminated, misstating the voter's ranking is unlikely to produce a more-preferred outcome — and may produce one that is less preferred.

On the other hand, IRV has some demerits. One issue is lack of verifiability. While, in principle, the reported outcome can be checked for errors and fraud, in fact comprehensive review is difficult and expensive and therefore rare. Governments have taken from three days to three weeks to process ranked ballots manually, often using a temporary work-force, and, naturally, they resist doing a recount. Computerization has reduced processing time to about three minutes, but manual verification then is difficult, especially if voters reported their rankings, not on paper ballots that were scanned, but by direct recording and/or online voting.

Another issue is Condorcet non-compliance. IRV may fail to elect a pairwise champion even though one is available. Tables 9a and 9b provides a real-world example. Bob Kiss was elected as the Mayor of Burlington Vermont in March 2009 with the sequence of tallies shown in Table 9a. However, Montroll won all five of his hypothetical paired comparisons — and therefore was a pairwise champion who did not win the election. These pairwise comparisons are shown in Table 9b.

Table 9a: Sequence of Tallies in the Election of the Mayor of Burlington, Vermont

Candidate	1st Tally	Hypothetical 2nd Tally	Hypothetical 3rd Tally	Actual 2nd Tally	Actual 3rd Tally
Bob Kiss (Progressive)	2585	2599	2606	2981	4313
Kurt Wright (Republican)	2951	2956	2963	3294	4061
Andy Montroll (Democrat)	2063	2067	2080	2554	–
Dan Smith (Independent)	1306	1315	1317	–	–
Write-ins	36	39	–	–	–
James Simpson (Green)	35	–	–	–	–
Total	8976	8976	8966	8829	8374
Eliminate	Simpson	Write-ins	Smith	Montroll	Wright

How often will IRV fail to elect an available pairwise champion? Merrill's simulation with 25 voters indicates that, with IRV (or Exhaustive Voting), that will happen in about 4% of elections with three candidates, 7% of elections with four candidates, 11% of elections with five candidates, 15% of elections with seven candidates, and 12% of elections with ten candidates. Those percentages are appreciably less than with runoff voting, but still well above zero.

Another deficiency of IRV is possible non-monotonicity, that is, the possibility that re-running an IRV election will deprive a candidate of victory even though the only difference between the two elections is that, in the re-run, some voters raise the rank of the candidate who won while making no change in the order in which they rank other candidates. Tables 10a–10c show how that perverse result can occur. Table 10a shows the preferences of the voters; note that, in the re-run, three voters raised Abe's rank while retaining the order of Ben, Cal, and Dee. Table 10b shows that with IRV and sincere voting, Abe wins the initial election. But Table 10c shows that, in the re-run where Abe has even higher ranks, the winner with IRV and sincere voting changes from Abe to Ben.

A real-world example also is available. After examining Burlington's 2009 mayoral

Table 9b: All Paired Comparisons of the Election of the Mayor of Burlington, Vermont

	Montroll	Kiss	Wright	Smith	Simpson	Write-in
Montroll	–	$4067 - 3477$ $= 590$	$4597 - 3668$ $= 929$	$4573 - 2998$ $= 1575$	$6267 - 591$ $= 5676$	$6658 - 104$ $= 6554$
Kiss	$3477 - 4067$ $= -590$	–	$4314 - 4064$ $= 250$	$3946 - 3577$ $= 369$	$5517 - 845$ $= 4672$	$6149 - 116$ $= 6033$
Wright	$3668 - 4597$ $= -929$	$4064 - 4314$ $= -250$	–	$3975 - 3793$ $= 182$	$5274 - 1309$ $= 3965$	$6063 - 163$ $= 5900$
Smith	$2998 - 4573$ $= -1575$	$3577 - 3946$ $= -369$	$3793 - 3975$ $= -182$	–	$5573 - 721$ $= 4852$	$6057 - 117$ $= 5940$
Simpson	$591 - 6267$ $= -5676$	$845 - 5517$ $= -4672$	$1309 - 5274$ $= -3965$	$721 - 5573$ $= -4852$	–	$3338 - 165$ $= 3173$
Write-ins	$104 - 6658$ $= -6554$	$116 - 6149$ $= -6033$	$163 - 6063$ $= -5900$	$117 - 6057$ $= -5940$	$165 + 3338$ $= -3173$	–

Table 10a: IRV Can Fail Monotonicity — Preferences of Voters

Ranking of Candidates	Number of Voters with that Ranking:	
	1st Election	Rerun Election
Abe >Ben >Cal >Dee	7	7
Ben >Abe >Cal >Dee	6	6
Cal >Ben >Abe >Dee	5	5
Dee >Cal >Ben >Abe	3	0
Dee >Abe >Cal >Ben	0	3
Total	21	21

Table 10b: IRV Can Fail Monotonicity — Initial Election Sequence of Tallies

Candidate	1st Tally	2nd Tally	3rd Tally
Abe	7	7	$7 + 6 = 13$
Ben	6	6	–
Cal	5	$5 + 3 = 8$	8
Dee	3	–	–
Total	21	21	21
Eliminate	Dee	Ben	Cal

Table 10c: IRV Can Fail Monotonicity — Rerun Election Sequence of Tallies

Candidate	1st Tally	2nd Tally	3rd Tally
Abe	7	$7 + 3 = 10$	10
Ben	6	6	$6 + 5 = 11$
Cal	5	5	–
Dee	3	–	–
Total	21	21	21
Eliminate	Dee	Cal	Abe

election, Gierzynski, Hamilton, and Smith determined that the winner would have changed from Kiss to Montroll if 753 voters who had ranked Wright above both Kiss and Montroll had, instead, ranked Kiss above Wright. If so, Wright would have been eliminated before (instead of after) Montroll, and then (by 4,067 to 3,755) Montroll would have defeated Kiss in the final tally.

4.4.6 Tactical Voting with IRV

Tactical Voting in an IRV election involves insincerely ranking the candidates. Doing so can produce a more-preferred outcome if the voter correctly anticipates the order in which candidates are eliminated. But, with the information normally available, that is difficult. Hence, tactical voting probably is rare in IRV elections.

4.4.7 Mandatory Truncation

In an IRV election in Maine or Ireland, a voter is free to rank as many or as few candidates as the voter wishes. In contrast, most American cities using IRV limit the number of candidates that a voter may rank.

IRV ballots in both the San Francisco Bay Area and Minneapolis, MN allow a voter to identify merely a first, a second, and a third choice. Because Oakland, CA has listed 10 candidates in a race for mayor, San Francisco has listed 16, and Minneapolis has listed 35, and because even one write-in uses up a choice, many ballots were "exhausted" before the final tally, that is, did not rank either the winner or the runner-up. That was true for 11% of the ballots in Oakland in 2010, 15% in San Francisco in 2011, and 20% in Minneapolis in 2013.

Undoubtedly, some of those ballots were exhausted, not because of Mandatory Truncation, but because there were more candidates than voters chose to rank. In the 2011 IRV election of the mayor of Portland, ME, the ballot permitted voters to rank all 15 named candidates, but at least 8.4% of the 19,634 valid ballots were exhausted by the final tally.

On the other hand, St. Paul allowed a voter to rank up to six candidates in its 2011 city-council election, and six was enough. Of 5,375 valid ballots for Ward 2's seat, 28% ranked one candidate, 32% ranked two, 23% ranked three, 7% ranked four, 6% ranked five, and 4% ranked all five listed candidates plus a write-in. Hence, the limit of six sufficed only because there were just five named candidates.

Mandatory Truncation can change the outcome. If the voters in our Table 3 had reported only their top three choices, the winner would have been, not Cal, but rather Abe (the plurality choice). With sincere voting, the sequence of tallies then would have been as shown in Table 11.

With Mandatory Truncation, however, sincere voting is an implausible assumption. Limiting voters to three choices deprives IRV of high resistance to tactical (that is, insincere) voting. In addition, Mandatory Truncation deprives IRV of an objective that

Table 11: Sequence of Tallies with Rank-3 IRV

Candidate	Number of Votes for That Candidate at:				
	Tally 1	Tally 2	Tally 3	Tally 4	Tally 5
Abe	10	10	10	10	10
Ben	5	5	5	6	–
Cal	4	5	8	8	8
Dee	3	4	4	–	–
Eve	3	3	–	–	–
Fay	2	–	–	–	–
None	0	0	0	3	9
Total	27	27	27	27	27
Eliminate	Fay	Eve	Dee	Cal	Ben

Tideman named "independence of clones."[6]

Equipment that can process more than three choices is available. Software used by the the city of Cambridge, Massachusetts, to implement single transferable vote (a multi-winner version of IRV) can accommodate as many candidates as the computer's memory allows. To date, however, no vendor has been willing to incur the expense of obtaining certification for such equipment in either California or Minnesota.

Lack of suitable equipment also produces delay. For example, in November 2013 election officials took more than 50 hours to determine Minneapolis' new mayor (Betsy Hodges)–and only then started tallying the hotly-contested city-council races.

4.4.8 Spoiled Ballots

A ballot — even from an eligible voter — is invalid ("spoiled") if the voter either "undervotes" or "overvotes". With simple plurality or runoff voting, "undervotes" means choosing no candidate for the seat, while "overvotes" means choosing two or more candidates. With IRV, similarly, "undervotes" means naming no first choice, while "overvotes" means naming more than one first choice. In either case, the ballot is ignored in the official tally.

Several other voting errors occur with IRV, but they invalidate only part of the ballot. (a) When a voter gives the same rank to more than one candidate, both the equal ranks and any lower ranks are not counted. (b) When a voter gives any candidate more than one rank,

---

[6]T. N. Tideman, "Independence of Clones as a Criterion for Voting Rules," Social Choice and Welfare, 4:185-206, 1987.

only the highest rank is counted. (c) When a voter skips a rank, lower-ranked candidates are moved up to fill the gap. These mistakes are surprisingly frequent (for example, they occurred on 15.1% of 79,462 ballots submitted in the 2013 election of Minneapolis' mayor), but they are laundered during tallying.

Because only an undervote or overvote will spoil an entire ballot, one might expect spoilage rates for IRV to be similar to spoilage rates for simple plurality or Top-2. The evidence, however, is ambiguous.

With simple plurality or Top-2, spoilage has varied widely from time to time. For example, spoilage rates in six recent elections were as follows: (1) 1.4% (France, 2007, 1st round — Sarkozy vs. Royal vs. Bayrou vs. Le Pen vs. 8 others); (2) 1.8% (U.S., 2000); (3) 2.2% (Mexico, 2000); (4) 2.5% (Taiwan, 2004); (5) 3.0% (Yugoslavia, 2000); (6) 4.2% (France, 2007 runoff — Sarkozy vs. Royal). The arithmetic average of these rates is 2.5%.

Spoilage in IRV elections compares favorably with those figures. In San Francisco's IRV race for mayor in 2011 (when Ed Lee defeated 15 other candidates), 1.4% of the 157,026 ballots were spoiled (0.47% were overvotes, and 0.93% were undervotes); and, in the 2011 IRV election of the mayor of Portland, ME (won by Michael Brennan), 2.9% of the 20,212 ballots were spoiled. Those rates average 2.2%.

Perhaps the best comparison of spoilage with and without IRV comes from presidential elections in the Republic of Ireland. The 1973 election (won by Erskine Childers) was, in effect, a plurality election because there were only two candidates. In that race, 0.56% of the 1,230,584 ballots were spoiled. The next contested elections were "real" IRV elections. In 1990 (when Mary Robinson defeated two other candidates), spoilage was 0.60%; in 1997 (when Mary McAleese defeated four other candidates), spoilage was 0.80%; and, in 2011 (when Michael Higgins defeated five other candidates), spoilage was 1.04%. Spoilage in these three elections averaged 0.8%, so it seems fair to say that spoilage in Ireland was higher when IRV was in effect — but still relatively low.

4.4.9 Spoilage in Australia

Spoilage in Australia is relatively high. From 1984 to 2010, there were ten elections to the national House of Representatives. Using IRV each time, each of 150 election districts chose one representative, and a total of about 12 million ballots were submitted. Spoilage ranged from 3.0% to 6.3%.

There seem to be three reasons for such high spoilage.

One reason is compulsory voting. Citizens 18 and older who, although not ill, abroad, etc., fail to sign in at a polling station face a fine of A\$20 (which, if contested, can become A\$50 plus costs). Since 1924, when voting became compulsory, 91%–96% of registered voters in fact have voted. However, some individuals resent the mandate and deliberately spoil their ballots.

A second reason for high spoilage in Australia is that Australian voters encounter three different election systems.

Many local elections use simple plurality (called, of course, "First Past the Post"). In addition, IRV (which Australians call "The Alternative Vote") is used every three years to elect both the national House of Representatives and the "lower" houses of five of Australia's six states.

Moreover, Australian voters encounter the single transferable vote (which Australians call "The Hare-Clark system"). With STV as with IRV, voters are invited to rank candidates, but each constituency elects more than one candidate. Every three years, each of Australia's six states and two territories uses STV to fill its seats in the national Senate, and six of those jurisdictions also use STV to elect one house in their state legislature.

Having more than one ballot design, more than one set of instructions, and more than one set of rules for determining the outcome — and perhaps, therefore, more than one voting strategy — is confusing, and the confusion probably increases both undervoting and overvoting.

A third reason for high spoilage in Australia is that voters encounter different rules concerning how many candidates a voter may or must rank.

4.4.10   Australia's Rules for Ranking

Voters participating in IRV and STV elections in Australia encounter four different rules concerning how many candidates a voter may or must rank.

One is a rule that Australians call "optional preferential voting". With it, a voter may rank as many or as few candidates as the voter wishes. This rule, however, applies only in the IRV elections to the lower house of New South Wales.

A second rule is called "Partial Preferential Voting". With it, a ballot is valid only if the voter ranks at least as many candidates as will be elected. This rule applies in STV elections to both the "lower" house of Tasmania and the unicameral legislature of Australian Capital Territory.

A third rule is called "full preferential voting". With it, a ballot is valid only if the voter ranks 100% of the candidates (however, if there are ten or more candidates — as often occurs — the 100% drops to at-least 90%). This rule applies in the IRV elections of both the national House of Representatives and the lower house of South Australia.

Australians call the remaining rule "full preferential voting with optional above-the-line voting". With this rule, a ballot is valid only if the voter either (a) ranks every candidate, or (b) chooses a party list ("group-voting ticket"). This rule applies in STV elections of the national Senate and of the "upper" houses of New South Wales, South Australia, Victoria, and Western Australia. (In practice, parties post and distribute their tickets, and over 96% of voters do vote "above the line", thereby producing the same winners as would emerge with a different multi-winner system, namely, the one called "closed-party lists".)

Of the voters who vote "below the line", many are "donkey voters", that is, voters who mindlessly rank candidates in whatever order they appear on the printed ballot. To minimize their influence, election officials use "Robson Rotation", that is, list candidates in different orders in different print-runs (a procedure introduced in Tasmania in 1979 by Neil Robson).

The last three rules are uniquely Australian. Since they entail mandatory ranking, they are a counterpart of the Mandatory Truncation found in American cities — and both kinds of restriction have dubious merit.

4.4.11   Compulsory Voting

In addition to Australia, according to Wikipedia, nine countries have and enforce compulsory voting: Argentina. Brazil, Congo, Ecuador, Luxembourg, Nauru, Peru, Singapore, and Uruguay. One might add North Korea, where 99% of voters loyally pick "yes" and the authorities see whether nonvoters are AWOL from the neighborhood or the country.

In addition, 14 other countries have compulsory voting but do not enforce it: Belgium, Bolivia, Costa Rica, Dominican Republic, Egypt, Greece, Honduras, Lebanon, Libya, Mexico, Panama, Paraguay, Thailand, and Turkey. Lack of enforcement probably lowers both turnout and spoilage.

4.5   Coombs System

4.5.1   How the System Selects the Winner

An election is held to fill one position. An official ballot lists individuals eligible to win the election, perhaps invites a write-in, and tells a voter to rank all of the candidates in order of preference. As in elections to Australia's national House of Representatives and the House of Assembly of South Australia, a submitted ballot is valid only if the voter ranks 100% of the candidates.

Qualified candidates initially receive one "vote" for each ballot on which they are first choice, and a candidate wins on the initial tally either (a) by receiving more than half of the votes tallied, or (b) by receiving exactly half and then winning a tie-break with another candidate who also received exactly half.

If no candidate wins on the initial tally, then officials identify the candidate who was ranked last by the largest number of voters (breaking a tie, if one occurred, randomly) and eliminate that candidate from contention.

Eliminating the straggler causes an adjustment. On any ballot where the eliminated candidate is ranked above at least one other candidate, each lower-ranked candidate advances one rank — for example, advances from second to first.

After the adjustment is made, officials make a second count of voters' top choices. As on the initial tally, a candidate wins either (a) by receiving more than half of the votes currently tallied, or (b) by receiving exactly half and then winning a tie-break with another candidate who also received exactly half.

If there is still no winner, officials continue eliminating, making the adjustment, and recounting until one of the candidates does either have more than half of the current vote-total or wins a tie-break with another candidate who also has exactly half.

4.5.2 Numerical Example

With the initial conditions shown in Table 3, six individuals, namely, Abe, Ben, Cal, Dee, Eve, and Fay, are eligible for a vacant seat and 27 persons are eligible to vote. If each eligible voter votes sincerely, then the ballots will show the rankings listed in Table 12a.

Table 12a: First Tally with Coombs System

| | Rank Assigned to Candidate: | | | | | | Number of Voters Assigning Those Ranks |
	Abe	Ben	Cal	Dee	Eve	Fay	
	1	2	5	3	4	6	6
	1	3	5	2	4	6	1
Precinct 1	1	5	4	3	6	2	3
	4	1	5	3	2	6	1
	6	1	5	4	3	2	4
	5	4	1	6	3	2	1
	6	5	1	4	3	2	3
Precinct 2	5	3	4	1	2	6	1
	5	4	6	1	2	3	1
	5	4	6	1	3	2	1
	5	4	3	6	1	2	1
	5	6	3	4	1	2	1
Precinct 3	6	5	3	4	1	2	1
	5	6	2	4	3	1	1
	5	6	4	2	3	1	1
					Total		27

In the initial tally, Abe, Ben, Cal, Dee, Eve, and Fay received 10, 5, 4, 3, 3, and 2 votes, respectively, the total being 27 votes.

Each of the candidates received fewer than half of the total of 27 votes, so no candidate wins on the initial tally.

Examining Table 12a, we see that Abe, Ben, Cal, Dee, Eve, and Fay were ranked last on 8, 3, 2, 2, 3, and 9 of the 27 ballots, respectively. Accordingly, Fay is now eliminated.

On 18 of the 27 ballots, Fay is ranked above at least one other candidate. On these 18 ballots, each of the lower-ranked candidates now moves up one rank.

With Fay eliminated and ranks adjusted accordingly, the ballots have the rankings shown in Table 12b.

Table 12b: Second Tally with Coombs System

		Rank Assigned to Candidate:					Number of Voters Assigning Those Ranks
	Abe	Ben	Cal	Dee	Eve	~~Fay~~	
	1	2	5	3	4	–	6
	1	3	5	2	4	–	1
Precinct 1	1	4	3	2	5	–	3
	4	1	5	3	2	–	1
	5	1	4	3	2	–	4
	4	3	1	5	2	–	1
	5	4	1	3	2	–	3
Precinct 2	5	3	4	1	2	–	1
	4	3	5	1	2	–	1
	4	3	5	1	2	–	1
	4	3	2	5	1	–	1
	4	5	2	3	1	–	1
Precinct 3	5	4	2	3	1	–	1
	4	5	1	3	2	–	1
	4	5	3	1	2	–	1
						Total	27

Candidates again receive one vote for each ballot on which they are now first choice, so Abe, Ben, Cal, Dee, and Eve now have 10, 5, 4, 3, and 5 votes, respectively. Still, each non-eliminated candidate has less than half of the votes cast and there is no winner.

Examining Table 12b, we see that Abe, Ben, Cal, Dee, and Eve were ranked last on 9, 3, 10, 2, and 3 of the 27 ballots, respectively. Accordingly, Cal is now eliminated and others' ranks are adjusted.

On 17 of the 27 ballots, Cal is ranked above at least one other candidate. On these 17 ballots, each of the lower-ranked candidates now moves up one rank.

With Cal eliminated and ranks adjusted accordingly, the ballots have the rankings shown in Table 12c.

Table 12c: Third Tally with Coombs System

	Rank Assigned to Candidate:						Number of Voters Assigning Those Ranks
	Abe	Ben	~~Cal~~	Dee	Eve	~~Fay~~	
	1	2	–	3	4	–	6
	1	3	–	2	4	–	1
Precinct 1	1	3	–	2	4	–	3
	4	1	–	3	2	–	1
	4	1	–	3	2	–	4
	3	2	–	4	1	–	1
	4	3	–	2	1	–	3
Precinct 2	4	3	–	1	2	–	1
	4	3	–	1	2	–	1
	4	3	–	1	2	–	1
	3	2	–	4	1	–	1
	3	4	–	2	1	–	1
Precinct 3	4	3	–	2	1	–	1
	3	4	–	2	1	–	1
	3	4	–	1	2	–	1
						Total	27

Candidates again receive one vote for each ballot on which they are now first choice, so Abe, Ben, Dee, and Eve now have 10, 5, 4, and 8 votes, respectively. Still, each non-eliminated candidate has less than half of the votes cast and there is no winner.

Examining Table 12c, we see that Abe, Ben, Dee, and Eve were ranked last on 12, 3, 2, and 10 of the 27 ballots, respectively. Accordingly, Eve is now eliminated and others' ranks are adjusted.

On 17 of the 27 ballots, Eve is ranked above at least one other candidate. On these 17 ballots, each of the lower-ranked candidates now moves up one rank.

With Eve eliminated and ranks adjusted accordingly, the ballots have the rankings shown in Table 12d.

Table 12d: Fourth Tally with Coombs System

		Rank Assigned to Candidate:					Number of Voters Assigning Those Ranks
	Abe	Ben	~~Cal~~	Dee	~~Eve~~	~~Fay~~	
	1	2	–	3	–	–	6
	1	3	–	2	–	–	1
Precinct 1	1	3	–	2	–	–	3
	3	1	–	2	–	–	1
	3	1	–	2	–	–	4
	2	1	–	3	–	–	1
	3	2	–	1	–	–	3
Precinct 2	3	2	–	1	–	–	1
	3	2	–	1	–	–	1
	3	2	–	1	–	–	1
	2	1	–	3	–	–	1
	2	3	–	1	–	–	1
Precinct 3	3	2	–	1	–	–	1
	2	3	–	1	–	–	1
	2	3	–	1	–	–	1
						Total	27

Candidates again receive one vote for each ballot on which they are now first choice, so Abe, Ben, and Dee now have 10, 7, and 10 votes, respectively. Still, each non-eliminated candidate has less than half of the votes cast and there is no winner.

Examining Table 12d, we see that Abe, Ben, and Dee were ranked last on 12, 7, and 8 of the 27 ballots, respectively. Accordingly, Abe is now eliminated and others' ranks are adjusted.

On 15 of the 27 ballots, Abe is ranked above at least one other candidate. On these 15 ballots, each of the lower-ranked candidates now moves up one rank.

With Abe eliminated and ranks adjusted accordingly, the ballots have the rankings shown in Table 12e.

Table 12e: Fifth Tally with Coombs System

| | Rank Assigned to Candidate: | | | | | | Number of Voters Assigning Those Ranks |
	Abe	Ben	Cal	Dee	Eve	Fay	
	–	1	–	2	–	–	6
	–	2	–	1	–	–	1
Precinct 1	–	2	–	1	–	–	3
	–	1	–	2	–	–	1
	–	1	–	2	–	–	4
	–	1	–	2	–	–	1
	–	2	–	1	–	–	3
Precinct 2	–	2	–	1	–	–	1
	–	2	–	1	–	–	1
	–	2	–	1	–	–	1
	–	1	–	2	–	–	1
	–	2	–	1	–	–	1
Precinct 3	–	2	–	1	–	–	1
	–	2	–	1	–	–	1
	–	2	–	1	–	–	1
						Total	27

Ben and Dee now have 13 and 14 votes, respectively, and the total is still 27. So at last — on the fifth tally — one of the candidates has more than half of the votes cast. That is Dee, who therefore wins the election.

It is not an accident that the winner in earlier sections was different — namely, Abe with simple plurality, Ben with runoff voting, Cal with unconstrained IRV, and now Dee with the Coombs system. Our numerical examples are designed to show that changing the election system, except between IRV and Exhaustive Voting, can change the winner even though voters' preferences do not change.

4.5.3 Who Uses the Coombs System

American psychologist Clyde Coombs devised the Coombs system in 1964.[7] Apparently the system has never been used, but it has attracted a little academic support.[8]

4.5.4 Tactical Voting with the Coombs system.

The Coombs system invites a voting tactic known as "burying". This involves insincerely lowering the rank of a candidate in order to cause that candidate to lose the election. With the Coombs system, the rank being lowered is lowered to last in order to eliminate that candidate.

For example, suppose that (a) a superintendent is to be elected, (b) Abe, Ben, and Cal are candidates, (c) the Coombs system will be used to determine the winner, (d) nine voters will submit valid ballots, and (e) the preference ordering is (i) Abe >Ben >Cal for voters *1*, *2*, *3*, and *4*, (ii) Ben >Abe >Cal for voters *5*, *6*, and *7*, and (iii) Cal >Ben >Abe for voters *8* and *9*. Then, with sincere voting, the number of first choices in the initial tally would be 4 for Abe, 3 for Ben, and 2 for Cal, and the number of last choices would be 2 for Abe, 0 for Ben, and 7 for Cal. Accordingly, Cal would be eliminated; votes received in the second tally would be 4 for Abe and 5 for Ben; and Ben would be elected.

However, suppose that voters *1*, *2*, *3*, and *4*, anticipating that outcome, rank the Abe >Cal >Ben on their ballots (instead of Abe >Ben >Cal), while the five other voters vote sincerely. Then, the number of first choices in the initial tally would be 4 for Abe, 3 for Ben, and 2 for Cal (as before), while the number of last choices now would be 2 for Abe, 4 for Ben, and 3 for Cal. Accordingly, Ben would be eliminated; votes received in the second tally now would be 7 for Abe and 2 for Cal; and the winner would change from Ben (the true second choice of voters *1*, *2*, *3*, and *4*) to Abe (their true first choice).

Since it is easy and obviously useful to rank the most competitive rival last, one should expect frequent use of the burying tactic if the Coombs system is ever adopted.

4.6 Borda System

4.6.1 How the System Selects the Winner

An election is held to fill one position. An official ballot lists individuals eligible to win the election, perhaps invites a write-in, and invites each voter to rank the candidates in order of preference, perhaps by assigning the number 1 to the candidate they most prefer, 2 to their second choice, 3 to their third choice, etc.

Being ranked first by a voter is worth a predetermined number of "points"; being ranked second is worth fewer points; being ranked third is worth still fewer; etc. For

---

[7]Clyde H. Coombs, A Theory of Data, New York, John Wiley and Sons, 1964.

[8]Bernard Grofman and Scott L. Feld, "If you like the Alternative Vote (a.k.a. the instant runoff), then you ought to know about the Coombs rule", Electoral Studies 23, 641–659, 2004.

example, being ranked first often is worth one point less than the number of candidates, being ranked second often is worth two points less than the number of candidates, etc. Whichever candidate has the largest total number of points wins the election — with a tie, if one occurs, being broken by lot.

4.6.2 Numerical Example

With the raw data in Table 3, six individuals, namely, Abe, Ben, Cal, Dee, Eve, and Fay, are eligible for a vacant seat and 27 persons are eligible to vote. If each eligible voter votes sincerely, then the ballots will show the rankings listed in Table 13a.

Table 13a: Ballots Received with Borda System

| | Rank Assigned to Candidate: | | | | | | Number of Voters Assigning Those Ranks |
	Abe	Ben	Cal	Dee	Eve	Fay	
	1	2	5	3	4	6	6
	1	3	5	2	4	6	1
Precinct 1	1	5	4	3	6	2	3
	4	1	5	3	2	6	1
	6	1	5	4	3	2	4
	5	4	1	6	3	2	1
	6	5	1	4	3	2	3
Precinct 2	5	3	4	1	2	6	1
	5	4	6	1	2	3	1
	5	4	6	1	3	2	1
	5	4	3	6	1	2	1
	5	6	3	4	1	2	1
Precinct 3	6	5	3	4	1	2	1
	5	6	2	4	3	1	1
	5	6	4	2	3	1	1
						Total	27

If being ranked first, second, third, fourth, fifth, or sixth is worth, respectively, 5, 4, 3, 2, 1, and no points, then the Borda counts are as shown in Table 13b.

Since Eve, with 74 points, has more points than any other candidate, Eve wins the election. In contrast, the winner was Abe with simple plurality, Ben with Runoff Voting, Cal with Exhaustive Voting and unconstrained IRV, and Dee with Coombs.

Table 13b: Borda Counts Using Traditional Weights

Candidate	Number of Points for That Candidate												
Abe	$10 \cdot 5$	+	$0 \cdot 4$	+	$0 \cdot 3$	+	$1 \cdot 2$	+	$8 \cdot 1$	+	$8 \cdot 0$	=	60
Ben	$5 \cdot 5$	+	$6 \cdot 4$	+	$2 \cdot 3$	+	$4 \cdot 2$	+	$7 \cdot 1$	+	$3 \cdot 0$	=	70
Cal	$4 \cdot 5$	+	$1 \cdot 4$	+	$3 \cdot 3$	+	$5 \cdot 2$	+	$12 \cdot 1$	+	$2 \cdot 0$	=	55
Dee	$3 \cdot 5$	+	$2 \cdot 4$	+	$10 \cdot 3$	+	$10 \cdot 2$	+	$0 \cdot 1$	+	$2 \cdot 0$	=	73
Eve	$3 \cdot 5$	+	$3 \cdot 4$	+	$11 \cdot 3$	+	$7 \cdot 2$	+	$0 \cdot 1$	+	$3 \cdot 0$	=	74
Fay	$2 \cdot 5$	+	$15 \cdot 4$	+	$1 \cdot 3$	+	$0 \cdot 2$	+	$0 \cdot 1$	+	$9 \cdot 0$	=	73

4.6.3   Who Uses the Borda System

The Borda system is named after French mathematician Jean-Charles de Borda. In 1770 he proposed that the French Academy of Sciences use a ranking ballot and point system to elect its members, and the Academy did so for about 20 years.[9]

Currently, the Borda system is used annually to select (a) the Most Valuable Player in Major League Baseball (14 points for first, 9 points for second, 8 for third, 7 for fourth, etc.), (b) the MVP in the National Basketball Association (10 points for first, 7 points for second, 5 for third, 3 for fourth, and 1 for fifth), (c) the NBA Rookie of the Year (5 points for first, 3 points for second, and 1 for third), (d) the NBA Coach of the Year (again 5 points for first, 3 points for second, and 1 for third), and (e) college football's Heisman Trophy winner (3 points for first, 2 points for second, and 1 for third). Most voters are sportswriters.

The Borda system also is used to select the winner of the world's most-watched non-sporting event. That is the Eurovision Song Contest. Every year since 1956, about 40 countries have entered contestants, and over 100 million viewers have watched them perform. The voters are countries, their rankings being determined 50% by a national jury and 50% by televoting. Being ranked first by a voter brings 12 points; second, 10 points; third, 8; fourth, 7; fifth, 6; sixth, 5; etc.

A Borda count also is used in some multi-winner elections. Every spring, 120 sportswriters and broadcasters choose three all-NBA teams. The ballot invites a voter to choose one center, two forwards, and two guards for each team, and a player receives 5 points for each first-team choice, 3 points for each second-team choice, and 1 point for each third-team choice. Five players win, namely, the player with the largest count received by a center, the two players with the largest and second-largest counts received by a forward, and the two players with the largest and second-largest counts received by a guard.

---

[9]Borda later published his method. See Jean-Charles, chevalier de Borda, "M'moire sur les élections au scrutin," in Histoire de l'Acad'mie Royale des Sciences, Paris, 1781.

Similarly, since 1971 the world's smallest independent republic, namely, Nauru (eight square miles, 10,000 people), has used a variation of the Borda system (locally called the "Dowdall system") when electing its parliament. In each of seven two-seat constituencies, the two candidates with the most total points are elected, and, in the one four-seat constituency, the four candidates with the most total points are elected.

Nauru's system gives relatively heavy weight to a first choice. Being ranked first by a voter brings 1 point; second, ½ point; third, ⅓ point; fourth, ¼ point; etc. As in parts of nearby Australia, Nauru requires "full preferential voting"; in other words, a ballot is valid only if the voter has ranked every candidate.

4.6.4 Importance of the Weights

What weights are used with the Borda system makes a difference. In our numerical example, being ranked first, second, third, fourth, fifth, or sixth was worth, respectively, 5, 4, 3, 2, 1, and 0 points, and Eve won. If, instead, being ranked first, second, third, fourth, fifth, or sixth is worth, respectively, 12, 10, 8, 7, 6, or 5 points (as in the Eurovision Song Contest), then Fay is the winner. Table 14 shows the associated Borda counts.

Table 14: Borda Counts Using Eurovision Weights

Candidate	Number of Points for That Candidate						
Abe	$10 \cdot 12$ +	$0 \cdot 10$ +	$0 \cdot 8$ +	$1 \cdot 7$ +	$8 \cdot 6$ +	$8 \cdot 5$ =	215
Ben	$5 \cdot 12$ +	$6 \cdot 10$ +	$2 \cdot 8$ +	$4 \cdot 7$ +	$7 \cdot 6$ +	$3 \cdot 5$ =	221
Cal	$4 \cdot 12$ +	$1 \cdot 10$ +	$3 \cdot 8$ +	$5 \cdot 7$ +	$12 \cdot 6$ +	$2 \cdot 5$ =	199
Dee	$3 \cdot 12$ +	$2 \cdot 10$ +	$10 \cdot 8$ +	$10 \cdot 7$ +	$0 \cdot 6$ +	$2 \cdot 5$ =	216
Eve	$3 \cdot 12$ +	$3 \cdot 10$ +	$11 \cdot 8$ +	$7 \cdot 7$ +	$0 \cdot 6$ +	$3 \cdot 5$ =	218
Fay	$2 \cdot 12$ +	$15 \cdot 10$ +	$1 \cdot 8$ +	$0 \cdot 7$ +	$0 \cdot 6$ +	$9 \cdot 5$ =	227

On the other hand, if being ranked first, second, third, fourth, fifth, or sixth is worth, respectively, 1, ½, ⅓, ¼, ⅕, or ⅙ point (as in Nauru), then Abe is the clear winner. The Borda counts then are as shown in Table 15.

As to what weights are best, there is, unfortunately, no right answer. As a result, there is also no single answer to which candidate the Borda system would elect.

4.6.5 Tactical Voting with the Borda system

Like the Coombs system, the Borda system invites the voting tactic called "burying". This involves insincerely lowering the rank of a candidate in order to cause that candidate to lose. For example, suppose that (a) a chairman is to be elected, (b) Abe, Ben, and Cal

Table 15: Borda Counts Using Nauru Weights

Candidate	Number of Points for That Candidate						
Abe	$10 \cdot 1$ +	$0 \cdot \frac{1}{2}$ +	$0 \cdot \frac{1}{3}$ +	$1 \cdot \frac{1}{4}$ +	$8 \cdot \frac{1}{5}$ +	$8 \cdot \frac{1}{6}$ =	13.2
Ben	$5 \cdot 1$ +	$6 \cdot \frac{1}{2}$ +	$2 \cdot \frac{1}{3}$ +	$4 \cdot \frac{1}{4}$ +	$7 \cdot \frac{1}{5}$ +	$3 \cdot \frac{1}{6}$ =	11.6
Cal	$4 \cdot 1$ +	$1 \cdot \frac{1}{2}$ +	$3 \cdot \frac{1}{3}$ +	$5 \cdot \frac{1}{4}$ +	$12 \cdot \frac{1}{5}$ +	$2 \cdot \frac{1}{6}$ =	9.5
Dee	$3 \cdot 1$ +	$2 \cdot \frac{1}{2}$ +	$10 \cdot \frac{1}{3}$ +	$10 \cdot \frac{1}{4}$ +	$0 \cdot \frac{1}{5}$ +	$2 \cdot \frac{1}{6}$ =	10.2
Eve	$3 \cdot 1$ +	$3 \cdot \frac{1}{2}$ +	$11 \cdot \frac{1}{3}$ +	$7 \cdot \frac{1}{4}$ +	$0 \cdot \frac{1}{5}$ +	$3 \cdot \frac{1}{6}$ =	10.4
Fay	$2 \cdot 1$ +	$15 \cdot \frac{1}{2}$ +	$1 \cdot \frac{1}{3}$ +	$0 \cdot \frac{1}{4}$ +	$0 \cdot \frac{1}{5}$ +	$9 \cdot \frac{1}{6}$ =	11.3

are candidates, (c) the Borda system is used to determine the winner, (d) being ranked first, second, or third is worth, respectively, 2, 1, and no points, (e) nine voters submit valid ballots, and (f) the preference ordering is (i) Abe >Cal >Ben for voters *1*, *2*, *3*, and *4*, (ii) Ben >Abe >Cal for voters *5*, *6*, and *7*, and (iii) Cal >Ben >Abe for voters *8* and *9*. Then, with sincere voting, points received would be $(4 \cdot 2) + (3 \cdot 1) = 11$ for Abe, $(3 \cdot 2) + (2 \cdot 1) = 8$ for Ben, and $(4 \cdot 1) + (2 \cdot 2) = 8$ for Cal. Hence, Abe would win.

However, suppose that voters *5*, *6*, and *7*, anticipating that outcome, rank the Ben >Cal >Abe on their ballots (instead of Ben >Abe >Cal), while other voters vote sincerely. Then points received would be $(4 \cdot 2) = 8$ for Abe, $(3 \cdot 2) + (2 \cdot 1) = 8$ for Ben, and $(4 \cdot 1) + (3 \cdot 1) + (2 \cdot 2) = 11$ for Cal — and the winner would change from Abe (the actual second choice of voters *5*, *6*, and *7*) to Ben (their actual first choice).

Since it is easy and obviously useful to rank the most competitive rival last, one should expect frequent use of the burying tactic when the Borda system is used — and anecdotal evidence supports that conjecture.

4.7 Bucklin System (also known as "Grand Junction Voting")

4.7.1 How the System Selects the Winner

An election is held to fill one position. An official ballot lists individuals eligible to win the election, perhaps invites a write-in, and asks each voter to rank the candidates in order of preference, perhaps by assigning the number 1 to the candidate they most prefer, 2 to their second choice, 3 to their third choice, etc.

If one of the candidates is first choice on more than half of the ballots, then that candidate wins the election. Otherwise, the candidate that is either first or second choice on the largest number of ballots wins, provided that candidate is either first or second choice on more than half of the ballots.

If no candidate is either first or second choice on more than half of the ballots, then include third choices. If necessary, continue including the next choice until at least one candidate does rank at or above that choice on more than half of the ballots — and therefore wins the election. Break a tie, if one occurs, by lot.

4.7.2 Numerical Example

With the initial conditions shown in Table 3, six individuals, namely, Abe, Ben, Cal, Dee, Eve, and Fay, are eligible for a vacant seat and 27 persons are eligible to vote. If each eligible voter votes sincerely, then the ballots will show the rankings listed in Table 16a.

Table 16a: Ballots Received with Bucklin System

	Rank Assigned to Candidate:						Number of Voters Assigning Those Ranks
	Abe	Ben	Cal	Dee	Eve	Fay	
	1	2	5	3	4	6	6
	1	3	5	2	4	6	1
Precinct 1	1	5	4	3	6	2	3
	4	1	5	3	2	6	1
	6	1	5	4	3	2	4
	5	4	1	6	3	2	1
	6	5	1	4	3	2	3
Precinct 2	5	3	4	1	2	6	1
	5	4	6	1	2	3	1
	5	4	6	1	3	2	1
	5	4	3	6	1	2	1
	5	6	3	4	1	2	1
Precinct 3	6	5	3	4	1	2	1
	5	6	2	4	3	1	1
	5	6	4	2	3	1	1
					Total		27

Consolidating the ballots, we obtain the sequence of Bucklin counts shown in Table 16b.

Table 16b: Bucklin Counts

Candidate	Number of voters who rank that candidate at or above:					
	1st	2nd	3rd	4th	5th	6th
Abe	10	10	10	11	19	27
Ben	5	11	13	17	24	27
Cal	4	5	8	13	25	27
Dee	3	5	15	25	25	27
Eve	3	6	17	24	24	27
Fay	2	17	18	18	18	27

With a total of 27 valid ballots, a Bucklin count of 14 or more is needed to win. None of the candidates is first choice on 14 or more ballots. On the other hand, one of the candidates, namely, Fay, is either first or second choice on 17 ballots. With the Bucklin system, therefore, the second tally produces a winner, namely, Fay.

Note that, although previous examples had the same initial conditions, they did not have the same outcome. The winner was (a) Abe with either Simple Plurality or rank-3 IRV, (b) Ben with Top-2, (c) Cal with either Exhaustive Voting or no-limit IRV, (d) Dee with the Coombs system, (e) depending on the weights used, any of several candidates with the Borda system, and now (f) Fay with the Bucklin system. As mentioned before, our numerical examples are designed to show that changing the election system, except between IRV and Exhaustive Voting, can change the winner even though voters' preferences do not change.

4.7.3   Who Uses the Bucklin System

From 1909 to 1922, about 50 American cities — including Cleveland, OH, San Francisco, CA, Jersey City, NJ, Denver, CO, and Spokane, WA — in 12 different states used the Bucklin system. The system is named after its designer, James Bucklin of Grand Junction, Colorado, the city where it was first used.[10]

The Bucklin system has intuitive appeal. If a majority of the voters rank a particular candidate first, then that candidate wins. Otherwise, the system takes second choices into account and produces a reasonable outcome — the Condorcet alternative — in the case where one of the candidates is every voter's second choice. That combination gives the Bucklin system relatively high — though not perfect — Condorcet efficiency.

---

[10]See James W. Bucklin, The Grand Junction Plan of City Government and Its Results, Annals of the American Academy of Political and Social Science, 38; 87–102, 1911.

Nevertheless, the system is no longer in use. Cities introduced voting machines in the early years of the 20th century, and the machines could not accommodate a ranking ballot. In addition, in 1915 the Minnesota supreme court held that, because a ballot provided multiple votes, the Bucklin system violated the state's constitution.[11] As a result, all of the cities using the Bucklin system soon abandoned it.

4.8 Majority Judgment

4.8.1 How the System Selects the Winner

An election is held to fill one position. An official ballot lists individuals eligible to win the election and perhaps invites a write-in. The ballot also lists a set of ratings — preferably six ratings, each being a word that is likely to have the same meaning to all voters — and tells a voter to assign one of those ratings to each candidate. The instructions may add that, if a voter does not assign a rating to a particular candidate, then the blank will be replaced by an average of other voters' ratings for that candidate.

Officials determine the median of each candidate's ratings, and the winner is the candidate whose median is highest.

4.8.2 Numerical Example

Let us again use the rankings shown in Table 3. Then six individuals, namely, Abe, Ben, Cal, Dee, Eve, and Fay, are eligible for a vacant seat and 27 persons are eligible to vote.

Suppose that (a) the voters are told to assign each candidate a grade in the set {*Excellent, Very Good, Good, Fair, Poor, Reject*}, (b) each voter assigns a different grade to each of the six candidates, and (c) each voter votes sincerely — in particular, assigning a grade of (i) *Excellent* to the candidate ranked first by that voter, (ii) *Very Good* to the candidate ranked second by that voter, (iii) *Good* to the candidate ranked third by that voter, (iv) *Fair* to the candidate ranked fourth by that voter, (v) *Poor* to the candidate ranked fifth by that voter, and (vi) *Reject* to the candidate ranked sixth by that voter. Table 17 shows the ratings that result.

The median rating (which happens to be *Very Good*) is highest for Fay, so Fay wins the election.

4.8.3 Who Uses Majority Judgment

French mathematicians Michel Balinski and Rida Laraki proposed Majority Judgment in 2006.[12] The system has received favorable reviews, but it is not — perhaps not yet

---

[11]Brown v. Smallwood, 130 Minn. 492, 153 N.W. 953 (1915).

[12]For the full treatment, see M. Balinski and R. Laraki, Majority Judgment: Measuring, Ranking, and Electing, MIT Press, 2010.

Table 17: Ratings Assigned to Candidates If Each Voter Gives Each Candidate a Different and Sincere Rating

		Rank Assigned to Candidate from the Set {Excellent, Very Good, Good, Fair, Poor, Reject}					Number of Voters Assigning Those Ranks
	Abe	Ben	Cal	Dee	Eve	Fay	
	Excellent	Very Good	Poor	Good	Fair	Reject	6
	Excellent	Good	Poor	Very Good	Fair	Reject	1
Precinct 1	Excellent	Poor	Fair	Good	Reject	Very Good	3
	Fair	Excellent	Poor	Good	Very Good	Reject	1
	Reject	Excellent	Poor	Fair	Good	Very Good	4
	Poor	Fair	Excellent	Reject	Good	Very Good	1
	Reject	Poor	Excellent	Fair	Good	Very Good	3
Precinct 2	Poor	Good	Fair	Excellent	Very Good	Reject	1
	Poor	Fair	Reject	Excellent	Very Good	Good	1
	Poor	Fair	Reject	Excellent	Good	Very Good	1
	Poor	Fair	Good	Reject	Excellent	Very Good	1
	Poor	Reject	Good	Fair	Excellent	Very Good	1
Precinct 3	Reject	Poor	Good	Fair	Excellent	Very Good	1
	Poor	Reject	Very Good	Fair	Good	Excellent	1
	Poor	Reject	Fair	Very Good	Good	Excellent	1
Median	Poor	Fair	Poor	Good	Good	Very Good	

— being used in public elections. The primary objections probably would be that (a) it would be difficult to confirm the absence of mistakes or fraud, and (b) the system is not Condorcet compliant (though like a Condorcet-compliant system, Majority Judgment is likely to elect a centrist).

4.8.4 Tactics with Majority Judgment

Majority Judgment invites use of a burying tactic, namely, giving the lowest allowed rating to a candidate whom the voter fears will defeat a candidate that the voter likes more or dislikes less. Conversely, Majority Judgment invites giving the highest allowed rating to whichever candidate the voter ranks first. Voters using this approach not only enhance the chances of their favorite but also tend to give their ballot more weight than the ballots of voters who do not exaggerate differences between candidates.

On the other hand, Balinski and Laraki reported that, in the simulated elections they studied, tactical voting changed the outcome less often with Majority Judgment than with various other election systems.

4.9 Schulze System (also known as "The Beatpath Method")

4.9.1 How the System Selects the Winner

An election is held to fill one position. An official ballot lists individuals eligible to win the election, perhaps invites a write-in, and invites each voter to rank the candidates in order of preference, perhaps by assigning the number 1 to the candidate they most prefer, 2 to their second choice, 3 to their third choice, etc.

The winner is determined in one of three ways.

First, if there is a Condorcet alternative (also called a "pairwise champion"), then that candidate wins. In other words, if voters' rankings imply that one of the candidates will receive more than half of the votes cast in a two-candidate runoff regardless of which of the other candidates also is in that runoff, then that candidate wins the election.

Second, if there is no Condorcet alternative, then apply "the beatpath criterion." It says that, if a majority of the voters prefer Abe to Ben, then Ben must not be elected unless there is a sequence of candidates from Ben to Abe wherein each candidate beats the next candidate with a majority that is at least as strong as the majority of Abe against Ben. If this criterion excludes all but one candidate, then that candidate wins the election.

Third, if (a) there is no Condorcet alternative, and (b) the beatpath criterion does not exclude all but one of the candidates, then choose one of the leading candidates either by lot or by another advanced procedure (such as Tideman's ranked-pairs method[13] or

---

[13]See (1) T. N. Tideman, "Independence of Clones as a Criterion for Voting Rules," Social Choice and Welfare, 4:185–206, 1987, and (2) T. M. Zavist and T. N. Tideman. "Complete independence of clones in the ranked pairs rule," Social Choice and Welfare , 6(2):167–173, 1989.

Stephen Eppley's maximize affirmed majorities[14]).

4.9.2 Numerical Example

With the raw data in Table 3, six individuals, namely, Abe, Ben, Cal, Dee, Eve, and Fay, are eligible for a vacant seat and 27 persons are eligible to vote. If each eligible voter votes sincerely, then the ballots will show the rankings listed in Table 18a.

Table 18a: Ballots Received with Schulze System

	Rank Assigned to Candidate:						Number of Voters Assigning Those Ranks
	Abe	Ben	Cal	Dee	Eve	Fay	
	1	2	5	3	4	6	6
	1	3	5	2	4	6	1
Precinct 1	1	5	4	3	6	2	3
	4	1	5	3	2	6	1
	6	1	5	4	3	2	4
	5	4	1	6	3	2	1
	6	5	1	4	3	2	3
Precinct 2	5	3	4	1	2	6	1
	5	4	6	1	2	3	1
	5	4	6	1	3	2	1
	5	4	3	6	1	2	1
	5	6	3	4	1	2	1
Precinct 3	6	5	3	4	1	2	1
	5	6	2	4	3	1	1
	5	6	4	2	3	1	1
						Total	27

Initially, we see whether there is a Condorcet alternative here. If so, that candidate wins the election. There will be four steps.

Step 1: Learn how many votes each candidate would receive if paired against each of the other candidates. The figures are shown in Table 18b. Each row in the table shows number of voters ranking that candidate over the candidates listed in each

---

[14]Eppley describes his system at http://wiki.electorama.com/wiki/Maximize_Affirmed_Majorities.

Table 18b: Votes for Each Candidate in Each of That Candidate's Paired Comparisons

	Abe	Ben	Cal	Dee	Eve	Fay
Abe	–	13	13	12	10	12
Ben	14	–	15	13	15	13
Cal	14	12	–	8	8	13
Dee	15	14	19	–	14	11
Eve	17	12	19	13	–	13
Fay	15	14	14	16	14	–

Table 18c: Margins of Victory and Defeat

	Margin of Victory/Defeat						Row Minimum
	Abe	Ben	Cal	Dee	Eve	Fay	
Abe	–	−1	−1	−3	−7	−3	−7
Ben	1	–	3	−1	3	−1	−1
Cal	1	−3	–	−11	−11	−1	−11
Dee	3	1	11	–	1	−5	−5
Eve	7	−3	11	−1	–	−1	−3
Fay	3	1	1	5	1	–	1

column. For example, 13 voters would vote for Abe over Ben but 14 for Ben over Abe.

Step 2: Determine (a) the margin of victory or defeat in each of the paired comparisons, (b) for each candidate, the minimum such margin, and (c) the maximin margin, that is, the largest of those minimum margins. The figures are shown in Table 18c. The margin of victory or defeat for Abe over Ben is the net of the number of voters who rank Abe over Ben (13) and the number of voters who rank Ben over Abe (14). Thus, the cell shows −1 for the margin of victory and defeat for Abe over Ben. Ben has defeated Abe by 1 vote. The Maximin (the largest of the row minima) is 1.

Step 3: See whether the maximin margin, that is, the largest number in the minimum column, is greater than 0. In this example, the maximin margin equals 1, which indeed is greater than 0. Hence, there is a Condorcet alternative here.

Step 4: If the maximin margin is greater than 0, then identify the candidate whose row contains the maximin margin. That candidate is a Condorcet alternative and therefore wins the election.

Here, the maximin margin is greater than 0, and it is in the row for Fay. That implies that, for each and every candidate other than Fay, more voters ranked Fay above the other candidate than ranked the other candidate above Fay. Hence, with the Schulze system, Fay wins the election. It is reasonable to think of Fay as an optimum — in particular, a Condorcet optimum, that is, an outcome that cannot be changed without displeasing more voters than are pleased.

As we have seen, the winner would be, not the Condorcet alternative, that is, Fay, but rather (a) Abe with either simple plurality or top-3 IRV, (b) Ben with Top-2, (c) Cal with either Exhaustive Voting or unconstrained IRV, (d) Dee with the Coombs system, (e) any of several candidates with the Borda system. Accordingly, it is evident that those election systems are not Condorcet compliant — and, although the Bucklin system and Majority Judgment did choose candidate Fay, they, too, may not choose an available Condorcet alternative.

4.9.3 Who Uses the Schulze System

German mathematician Markus Schulze developed the Schulze system at the Technische Universitat Berlin in 1997. He later described it in a journal article.[15]

At present, all users are non-governmental entities. They include Northwestern University's student government (3,471 valid ballots for president in April 2013), Wikimedia

---

[15]M. Schulze, "A new Monotonic, Clone-Independent, reversal symmetric, and Condorcet-consistent Single-Winner Election Method, " Social Choice and Welfare, 36:267-303, 2011.

Foundation (3,368 valid ballots in June 2011), Pirate Party of Sweden (50,000 members), Free Software Foundation Europe (900 members), Debian (900), Squeak (500), Software in the Public Interest (400), Gentoo (300), and SUNY Graduate Student Organization (300). Plus about 50 smaller organizations.

The first part of Schulze's criterion for choosing the winner, that is, awarding victory to a Condorcet alternative if there is one, was widely recommended long before 1997. For example, the writer who launched the modern theory of elections, namely Scottish economist Duncan Black, advocated that rule.[16]

Schulze's contribution was the second part of his method for choosing a winner. It provided a new way to determine the winner when there is no Condorcet alternative, that is, a new way to decide which member of a group of imperfect candidates is least bad. Such methods are called "Condorcet-completion rules."

Condorcet-completion had been controversial for decades. Black's answer was to use a Borda count. Other writers had proposed completing with IRV. But all suggestions had deficiencies compared to Schulze's proposal. As a result, Schulze's work quickly received international acclaim.

4.9.4   Numerical Example with No Condorcet Alternative

The Schulze system selects a winner when there is no Condorcet alternative, that is, when, by majority rule, each of the candidates loses or ties in at least one of that candidate's paired comparisons. This can occur because different voters constitute the majority in different comparisons To illustrate that case, we need a second numerical example.

Assume, this time, that five individuals, namely, Abe, Ben, Cal, Dee, and Eve, are eligible for a vacant seat, 45 voters submit a valid ballot, and the ballots have the rankings shown in Table 19a.

We will determine the winner in seven steps, the first three steps being the same as with our first example.

Step 1: See how many votes each candidate would receive if paired against each of the other candidates. Table 19b shows the figures.

Step 2: Determine (a) the margin of victory or defeat in each of the paired comparisons, (b) for each candidate, the minimum such margin, and (c) the maximin margin, that is, the largest of those minimum margins. Table 19c shows the figures. The Maximin is -3.

Step 3: See whether the maximin margin, that is, the largest number in the minimum column, is greater than 0. In this example, the maximin margin equals -3, which is not greater than 0.

---

[16]Duncan Black, The Theory of Committees and Elections, Cambridge University Press, 1958.

Table 19a: Ballots Received in the Second Schulze Numerical Example

	\multicolumn{5}{c}{Rank Assigned to Candidate:}	Number of Voters Assigning Those Ranks
	Abe	Ben	Cal	Dee	Eve	
Precinct 1	1	3	2	5	4	5
	1	5	4	2	3	5
	4	1	5	3	2	8
	2	3	1	5	4	3
Precinct 2	2	4	1	5	3	7
	3	2	1	4	5	2
	5	4	2	1	3	7
	3	2	5	4	1	8
					Total	45

Table 19b: Votes for Each Candidate in Each of That Candidate's Paired Comparisons in Second Schulze Numerical Example

	Abe	Ben	Cal	Dee	Eve
Abe	–	20	26	30	22
Ben	25	–	16	33	18
Cal	19	29	–	17	24
Dee	15	12	28	–	14
Eve	23	27	21	31	–

Table 19c: Margins of Victory and Defeat in Second Schulze Numerical Example

| | Margin of Victory/Defeat | | | | | Row Minimum |
	Abe	Ben	Cal	Dee	Eve	
Abe	–	−5	7	15	−1	−5
Ben	5	–	−13	21	−9	−13
Cal	−7	13	–	−11	3	−11
Dee	−15	−21	11	–	−17	−21
Eve	1	9	−3	17	–	−3

When, as here, the maximin margin is less than 0, there is, for every candidate, at least one other candidate ranked higher by more voters than rank that other candidate lower. Hence, with majority rule, each of the candidates loses at least one of its paired comparisons, and there is no Condorcet alternative.

Because each candidate loses at least one of its paired comparisons, "voting cycles", that is, inconsistent rankings emerge as follows:

By majority rule, (Abe >Cal) and (Cal >Ben >Abe), producing the cycle (Abe >Cal >Ben >Abe).

By majority rule, (Ben >Dee) and (Dee >Cal >Ben), producing the cycle (Ben >Dee >Cal >Ben).

By majority rule, (Cal >Eve) and (Eve >Dee >Cal), producing the cycle (Cal >Eve >Dee >Cal).

By majority rule, (Dee >Cal) and (Cal >Ben >Dee), producing the cycle (Dee >Cal >Ben >Dee).

By majority rule, (Eve >Ben) and (Ben >Abe >Cal >Eve), producing the cycle (Eve >Ben >Abe >Cal >Eve).

Given these contradictions, not even a partial ordering of the candidates emerges. That this can happen even though each voter individually has a complete and transitive ranking of the candidates is known as "Condorcet's paradox of voting."

Because there is no Condorcet alternative here, we proceed to a new Step 4.

Step 4: For each pair of candidates, such as Abe and Ben, do the following three things:

(a) Identify all beatpaths from Abe to Ben, that is, all chains of two or more paired comparisons in which Abe, by receiving more than half of the votes cast, beats another candidate (possibly Ben) in the first comparison, the loser of which (if not Ben), by receiving more than half of the votes cast, wins the next comparison, and so on until the loser of the last comparison is Ben.

(b) Determine the "strength" of each such beatpath (that is, the fewest votes for the winner in any paired comparison in that chain).

(c) Identify the strongest such beatpath. These are shown in Table 19d. Each row contains the strongest beatpath from that candidate to the one listed in each column.

Showing 4c, but not 4a or 4b, we have, for the strongest beatpaths from each candidate to each other candidate, the paths shown in Table 19d.

Table 19d: Strongest Beatpaths in Second Schulze Numerical Example

	Abe	Ben	Cal	Dee	Eve
Abe	–	A >D >C >B	A >D >C	A >D	A >D >C >E
Ben	B >A	–	B >D >C	B >D	B >D >C >E
Cal	C >B >A	C >B	–	C >B >D	C >E
Dee	D >C >B >A	D >C >B	D >C	–	D >C >E
Eve	E >D >C >B >A	E >D >C >B	E >D >C	E >D	–

Step 5: For every pair of candidates, determine the strength of the strongest beatpath from each of those two candidates to the other. Here the strongest beatpaths (which were identified in the previous step) have the strengths shown in Table 19e.

Table 19e: Strength of Strongest Beatpath in Second Schulze Numerical Example

	Abe	Ben	Cal	Dee	Eve
Abe	–	28	28	30	24
Ben	25	–	28	33	24
Cal	25	29	–	29	24
Dee	25	28	28	–	24
Eve	25	28	28	31	–

Step 6: Determine (a) for each pair of candidates, the difference between (i) the strength of the strongest beatpath from one candidate to the other, and (ii) the strength of the strongest beatpath back to the first candidate, (b) for each candidate individually, the minimum such difference, and (c) the maximin difference, that is, the largest of those minimum differences. Table 19f shows these figures. The Maximin is 1.

Table 19f: Difference in Strength for Each Pair of Strongest Beatpaths in Second Schulze Numerical Example

| | Strength of the Strongest Beatpath | | | | | Row Minimum |
	Abe	Ben	Cal	Dee	Eve	
Abe	–	3	3	5	−1	−1
Ben	−3	–	−1	5	−4	−4
Cal	−3	1	–	1	−4	−4
Dee	−5	−5	−1	–	−7	−7
Eve	1	4	4	7	–	1

Step 7: Identify the candidate(s) whose row(s) contain the maximin strength, breaking a tie, if one occurs, either by Tideman's ranked-pairs method or by chance. In this example, there is no tie; the maximin strength belongs only to Eve, and Eve therefore wins the election.

As the foregoing example indicates, Schulze's Condorcet-completion rule is complicated. However, as Table 23 below (a table that compares the various single-winner systems) indicates, there is compensation, namely, mutual-majority compliance, monotonicity, independence of clones, vote once, and sincere voting.

4.9.5 Cornell's Condorcet Internet Voting Service

Anyone can arrange for an election that will award victory to a Condorcet alternative if there is one. Since 2003, more than 70,000 votes have been cast in more than 3,000 elections run by the Condorcet Internet Voting Service (CIVS), a free Internet voting service offered by Andrew Myers at the Cornell Computer Science Department.[17] CIVS has been used by plant fanciers, sports teams, book clubs, music lovers, prom organizers, beer drinkers, fraternities, church groups, PBeM gamers — and even by families naming pets and children.

---

[17]CIVS is at http://www.cs.cornell.edu/andru/civs.html.

For Condorcet-completion, CIVS will implement both the Schulze criterion and three other rules (namely, Condorcet-IRV and two ranked-pairs methods). If you are lucky, all four methods will produce the same answer.

4.9.6   Tactical Voting with the Schulze System

With the Schulze system, voters can obtain a more preferred outcome by compromising or burying, provided a voting cycle exists or can be created. The compromising tactic involves ranking a less-preferred candidate above a more-preferred candidate in order to help defeat a disliked third candidate, and the burying tactic involves ranking a disliked candidate below a candidate who, although disliked even more, is unlikely to win. However, with the information normally available, implementation is difficult and therefore seems unlikely.

4.9.7   Effect on Ballot

Because the Schulze system determines the winner without counting how many first choices each candidate received, its ranking ballot can differ from the ranking ballot used with instant-runoff voting or with the Coombs, Borda, or Bucklin systems. Two differences are especially noteworthy.

First, a voter can be allowed to assign the same rank to more than one candidate. That voter's ballot will be ignored when comparing the equally-ranked alternatives but counted when comparing one of the equally-ranked alternatives with some other alternative. With Instant-Runoff, Coombs, Borda, or Bucklin, in contrast, a ballot naming more than one first choice is invalid.

Second, one of the alternatives offered to voters can be "none-of-the-above" or — as in every statewide election in Nevada since 1975 — "None of these candidates." If that is done and a named candidate wins, then you can infer that the winner is, not only preferred to the other named candidates, but also favored enough to be (say) hired. Conversely, if "None" wins the election, then you might conclude that none of the named candidates should be hired.

In fact, the Debian Project (an association of individuals dedicated to developing and distributing free software) does include the none option when developers, using the Schulze system, choose a project leader. Section 5.2.6 of the Debian Constitution of 2007 says, "The options on the ballot will be those candidates who have nominated themselves and have not yet withdrawn, plus none-of-the-above. If none-of-the-above wins the election then the election procedure is repeated, many times if necessary."[18]

---

[18]See https://www.debian.org/devel/constitution.

4.9.8 Black's Single-Peakedness theorem

One of Duncan Black's contributions is known as the single-peakedness theorem.[19] It tells us when there surely will be a Condorcet alternative. I paraphrase the theorem as follows:

> If voters' rankings are complete and transitive, and also are (as defined in the next paragraph) "single peaked" for at least one ordering of the candidates, then pairwise comparisons with majority rule will produce a complete and transitive ordering of the candidates, that is, an array without voting cycles and therefore with an unambiguous social first-choice.

Voters' rankings are "single-peaked" for a particular ordering of the candidates if, when the candidates are positioned horizontally in that order (such as from very conservative to very progressive), then (a) for every voter, none of the candidates is located between two other candidates that that voter ranks higher, and (b) for any two candidates that either are both right of or are both left of any voter's first choice, that voter prefers whichever of the two is closer to that voter's first choice — and therefore a graph of any voter's ratings of the candidates has no valleys, only a single peak over the most-left or the most-right candidate or over a candidate somewhere between them.

For example, assume that there are three candidates, namely, Abe, Ben, and Cal, and three voters, namely, *1*, *2*, and *3*, and that voter *1* ranks Ben >Abe >Cal, while voter *2* ranks Abe >Cal >Ben, and voter *3* ranks Cal >Abe >B. With those rankings, voters' preferences are single-peaked if we place Abe between Ben and Cal — that is, if we order the candidates either Ben-Abe-Cal or Cal-Abe-Ben. With either of those orderings, Abe is located between two other candidates, but no voter ranks both of the other candidates higher than Abe. Also, Abe is closer than Cal to voter *1*'s first choice (namely, Ben) and is preferred to Cal by *1*; similarly, Abe is closer than Ben to voter *3*'s first choice (namely, Cal) and is preferred to Ben by *3*.

In this example, consequently, majority rule will, given sincere voting, produce a complete and transitive ordering of the candidates. In particular, a 2-to-1 majority (namely, voter *2* and voter *3*) would rank Abe above Ben; a 2-to-1 majority (namely, *1* and *2*) would rank Abe above Cal; and a 2-to-1 majority (namely, *2* and *3*) would rank Cal above Ben. Hence, a full and internally consistent social ranking would emerge, namely, Abe >Cal >B.

Do not infer that, absent single-peaked preferences, pairwise comparisons with majority rule will not produce a social first-choice. For instance, the rankings in our Table 3 are not single-peaked, but the paired comparisons, nevertheless, yield a complete and transitive social ordering of the six candidates, namely, Fay >Dee >Ben >Eve >Cal >Abe. In other words, single-peakedness is sufficient but not necessary.

---

[19]Duncan Black, "On the Rationale of Group Decision-Making", Journal of Political Economy 56: 23'34, 1948.

4.9.9 Black's Median-Voter Theorem

Another contribution of Duncan Black is known as the median-voter theorem. It tells us why a Condorcet-compliant election system, such as Schulze's system, tends to elect a centrist (such as Burlington's Andy Montroll). I paraphrase the theorem as follows:

Suppose that (a) voters' preferences for a particular set of three or more candidates are single-peaked (in the sense defined above) for a particular ordering of the candidates, (b) when the candidates are arrayed in that order, the number of voters whose first choice is to the left of one of the candidates is the same as the number of voters whose first choice is to the right of that candidate, and (c) that candidate (the "median candidate") also is the first choice of at least one voter (a "median voter"), Then, with sincere voting, the first choice of a median voter, that is, the centrist candidate, would obtain a majority of the votes cast in a runoff against any of the other candidates — and therefore win the election if the election system is Condorcet compliant.

Do not infer that, if voters' preferences are not single-peaked, then a Condorcet-compliant election system will not select a candidate at the political center. Single-peaked preferences are sufficient, but not necessary, to cause a Condorcet-compliant election system to produce a centrist winner.

4.10 Maximin system (also called "the Minimax system" and "the Simpson-Kramer method")

4.10.1 How the System Selects the Winner

An election is held to fill one position. An official ballot lists individuals eligible to win the election and invites each voter to rank the candidates in order of preference, perhaps by assigning the number 1 to the candidate they most prefer, 2 to their second choice, 3 to their third choice, etc. The ballot may add "none-of-the-above" to the list of candidates and also may invite a write-in.

The winner is determined in one of three ways.

First, if there is a Condorcet alternative, then that candidate wins. That is, if voters' rankings imply that one of the candidates would receive more than half of the votes cast in a two-candidate runoff, regardless of which of the other candidates also was in that runoff, then that candidate wins the election. To see whether there is a Condorcet alternative, proceed as with the Schulze system, that is:

1. See how many votes each candidate would receive if paired against each of the other candidates in a runoff election.

2. For each candidate, determine the margin of victory or defeat (that is, the number of favorable votes less the number of unfavorable votes) in each of that candidate's paired comparisons.

3. See whether, for one of the candidates, every margin is greater than 0.

4. If, for one of the candidates, every margin is greater than 0, then that candidate is a Condorcet alternative and wins the election.

Second, if there is no Condorcet alternative, but the worst margin in paired comparisons is least bad for exactly one of the candidates, then that candidate wins. In other words, if the most negative difference between favorable votes and unfavorable votes in two-candidate runoffs is less negative for one candidate than for any of the other candidates, then that candidate wins the election.

Third, if (a) there is no Condorcet alternative, and (b) the worst margin in paired comparisons is the same for two or more of the candidates, then choose one of the tied candidates by lot. For example, if two candidates would win a runoff against any of the other candidates but tie in a runoff against each other, then the worst margin for both of those candidates is 0, and the tie would be broken by chance.

4.10.2 Numerical Example

The first part of both the Maximin rule and Schulze's rule say that, when one of the candidates is a Condorcet alternative, that candidate wins the election. Hence, with the first example used above, the Maximin system would elect the same candidate as the Schulze system, namely, Fay. Moreover, the calculations leading to that conclusion are identical.

To illustrate Condorcet completion with the Maximin system, therefore, I will refer the second example used to illustrate the Schulze system, that is, the example with no Condorcet alternative.

Assume again that five individuals, namely, Abe, Ben, Cal, Dee, and Eve, are eligible for a vacant seat; 45 voters submit a valid ballot; and the ballots have rankings shown in Table 20a.

We will determine the winner in three steps.

Step 1: See how many votes each candidate would receive if paired against each of the other candidates. Table 20b shows the figures.

Step 2: Determine (a) the margin of victory or defeat in each of the paired comparisons, (b) for each candidate, the minimum such margin, and (c) the maximin margin, that is, the largest of those minimum margins. Table 20c shows the figures.

Table 20a: Ballots Received in the Second Schulze Numerical Example

| | Rank Assigned to Candidate: | | | | | Number of Voters Assigning Those Ranks |
	Abe	Ben	Cal	Dee	Eve	
Precinct 1	1	3	2	5	4	5
	1	5	4	2	3	5
	4	1	5	3	2	8
	2	3	1	–	4	3
Precinct 2	2	4	1	5	3	7
	3	2	1	4	5	2
	5	4	2	1	3	7
	3	2	5	4	1	8
					Total	27

Table 20b: Votes for Each Candidate in Each of That Candidate's Paired Comparisons in Second Schulze Numerical Example

	Abe	Ben	Cal	Dee	Eve
Abe	–	20	26	30	22
Ben	25	–	16	33	18
Cal	19	29	–	17	24
Dee	15	12	28	–	14
Eve	23	27	21	31	–

Table 20c: Margins of Victory and Defeat in Second Schulze Numerical Example

| | Margin of Victory/Defeat | | | | | Row Minimum |
	Abe	Ben	Cal	Dee	Eve	
Abe	–	−5	7	15	−1	−5
Ben	5	–	−13	21	−9	−13
Cal	−7	13	–	−11	3	−11
Dee	−15	−21	11	–	−17	−21
Eve	1	9	−3	17	–	−3

Step 3: Lastly, identify the candidate(s) whose row(s) contain the maximin margin, that is, the row(s) containing the largest number in the minimum column. If one candidate has the maximin margin, then that candidate wins the election. If two or more candidates have the maximin margin, then choose one of them by chance.

Here, there is no tie. The maximin margin, namely, −3, is in candidate Eve's row. Hence, Eve is the winner.

Note that, with the maximin criterion, unlike the Schulze criterion, the maximin margin determines the winner whether or not that maximin is greater than 0. If the maximum margin is greater than 0, then the winner is a Condorcet alternative. If the maximin margin is less than 0, then the winner is the candidate whose worst margin is least bad. If the maximin margin is exactly 0, then the winner is the candidates whose worst margins is 0 who wins a tie-breaker.

In this example, the maximin margin in fact is less than 0. Hence, for every candidate, there is at least one other candidate ranked higher by more voters than rank that other candidate lower. With majority rule, consequently, each of the candidates loses at least one of its paired comparisons and, as shown earlier, those losses produce voting cycles, that is, inconsistent social rankings.

According to the maximin criterion, those cycles do the least damage to candidate Eve. Having Eve win will minimize the maximum difference between the number of voters who could be pleased by changing the winner and the number of voters whom that change would displease. In particular, making Eve the winner will hold that maximum difference down to three. Put differently, if Eve is the winner, then the number of additional voters, all favoring the winner, needed to make the winner be a Condorcet alternative is as small as possible, namely, merely four.

As seen above, Eve would win with the Schulze system as well as with the Maximin-maximin system. Eve also would win with the Coombs system. With the other systems described earlier, however, the result would be different. Plurality, Exhaustive, no-limit

IRV, and Bucklin would choose Cal. Top-2 would elect Abe.

Do not infer that Maximin and Schulze will always pick the same winner. Maximin fails a desideratum called "the mutual majority criterion" (also known as "the generalized majority criterion"), while Schulze (along with instant-runoff voting and Bucklin) pass it. This criterion states that, if there is a subset of the candidates such that more than half of the voters strictly prefer every member of the subset to every candidate outside the subset, then the winner must come from the subset. (For Condorcet compliance, which is sometimes called "the majority criterion", the winner must come from that subset only if the subset contains exactly one candidate.)

4.10.3 Who Uses Maximin

No users yet.

4.11 Approval Voting

4.11.1 How the System Selects the Winner

An election is held to fill one position. An official ballot lists individuals eligible to win the election, perhaps invites a write-in, and tells a voter to use the checkboxes next to the candidates' names to approve as many candidates as the voter wishes.

Whichever candidate is approved on the largest number of valid ballots wins the election — provided, perhaps, that a majority or supermajority of voters have approved that candidate. Officials break a tie, if one occurs, by lot.

4.11.2 Numerical Example

With the initial conditions shown in Table 3, six individuals, namely, Abe, Ben, Cal, Dee, Eve, and Fay, are eligible for a vacant seat and 27 persons are eligible to vote. Suppose that the voters vote sincerely — which, with approval voting, means both that a voter who approves of a particular candidate also approves of every candidate whom that voter ranks above the approved candidate, and that a voter who does not approve of a particular candidate also does not approve of any candidate whom that voter ranks below the unapproved candidate (conversely, insincere approval voting means either not approving a candidate whom the voter ranks above a candidate whom that voter does approve or approving a candidate whom the voter ranks below a candidate whom that voter does not approve).

The outcome depends on how many candidates each voter approves. We will consider six possibilities: (1) each voter approves just one candidate; (2) each voter approves two candidates; (3) each voter approves three candidates; (4) each voter in Precinct 1 approves one candidate, each voter in Precinct 2 approves two candidates, and each voter in Precinct

3 approves three candidates; (5) the number of candidates approved by a voter is three in Precinct 1, two in Precinct 2, and one in Precinct 3; and (6) the number of candidates approved by a voter is three in Precinct 1, one in Precinct 2, and two in Precinct 3. Table 21 shows what happens in each of these six cases.

Table 21: Outcome with Approval Voting

	Case 1	Case 2	Case 3	Case 4	Case 5	Case 6
Abe	10	10	10	10	10	10
Ben	5	11	13	6	12	12
Cal	4	5	8	4	4	5
Dee	3	5	15	3	14	15
Eve	3	6	17	10	10	8
Fay	2	17	18	8	14	12
Total	27	54	81	41	64	62
Plurality Winner	Abe	Fay	Fay	Abe, Eve	Dee, Fay	Dee
Majority Winner	–	Fay	Fay	–	Dee, Fay	Dee

The number of candidates approved by a voter is:
Case 1: 1 in each precinct
Case 2: 2 in each precinct
Case 3: 3 in each precinct
Case 4: 1 in Precinct 1, 3 in Precinct 2, 1 in Precinct 3
Case 5: 3 in Precinct 1, 2 in Precinct 2, 1 in Precinct 3
Case 6: 3 in Precinct 1, 1 in Precinct 2, 2 in Precinct 3

As Table 21 indicates, the outcomes vary from case to case. If a candidate needs approvals from a majority of the voters to win, then no candidate wins in Cases 1 and 4, Fay wins in Cases 2 and 3, Dee or Fay wins in Case 5, and Dee wins in Case 6. If a majority is not required, then the winner is Abe in Case 1, Fay in Cases 2 and 3, Abe or Eve in Case 4, Dee or Fay in Case 5, and Dee in Case 6. Unfortunately, there is no objectively correct way to decide how many candidates to approve, and small changes in the number chosen can change the outcome.

4.11.3 Who Uses Approval Voting

Approval voting was proposed by American writer Guy Ottewell in 1968, named by American economist Robert Weber in 1977, and elaborated by American political scientist

Steven Brams and American mathematician Peter Fishburn in 1978.[20]

Approval voting has attracted attention. Users include the Mathematical Association of America, Institute for Operations Research and Management Sciences, American Statistical Association, and the Dartmouth student government. Approval also is used in electing the Secretary General of the United Nations; before the Security Council votes formally, several rounds of approval voting seek a consensus.

An approval system can be implemented sequentially as well as simultaneously. For example, in February 2011, when the city council of Davis, CA, replaced a resigned member, each of the four continuing members (1) indicated approval of four of the ten applicants, and the number of candidates then was reduced from ten to the seven who received at least two approvals; (2) indicated approval of three of those seven, and the number of candidates then was reduced to the four who again received at least two approvals; (3) indicated approval of two of those four, and the number of candidates then was reduced to the three who again received at least two approvals; and (4) indicated approval of two of those three, and the number of candidates then was reduced to the two who received at least three approvals. Finally, on a 3-to-1 vote, one of those two finalists (Dan Wolk) was elected.

An approval system can also be used when two or more candidates will be — or may be — elected. Here are several examples:

Long-term members of the Baseball Writers' Association of America are invited to vote for up to ten candidates for the National Baseball Hall of Fame, and every candidate approved on at least 75% of the valid ballots is elected. A screening committee nominates the candidates (37 were nominated in 2013).

The Pro Football Hall of Fame has somewhat different rules. In three rounds of email voting, a selection committee narrows the list of candidates to 17 finalists. Then, at an in-person meeting the day before the Super Bowl, the top four vote-getters win, as do up to three other finalists if they have been approved by at least 80% of the voters.

At Princeton University, the undergraduate student government elects (a) for class senators, the two candidates with the largest number of approvals, and (b) for U-Council, the ten candidates with the most approvals. If a tie occurs, a runoff election is held the following week.

4.11.4 Tactics with Approval Voting

Approval voting can reward tactical voting. One likely tactic is compromising. Here, that involves giving approval to a candidate whom the voter dislikes (along with all candidates that the voter ranks higher) in order to defeat a candidate whom the voter dislikes even more and fears will be elected. Conversely, it is reasonable for a voter to withhold approval of acceptable candidates whom the voter fears will defeat a candidate that the

---

[20]S. Brams and P. Fishburn, "Approval Voting." American Political Science Review 72 (3): 831'847 (1978).

voter likes even more. These tactics are rather obvious and therefore are likely to occur in practice.

That these tactics are available also creates emotional resistance to approval voting. Voters dislike having to decide whether to jeopardize a more-preferred candidate by also approving a less-preferred — but not disliked — candidate. In addition, voters dislike being unable to rank one approved or not-approved candidate above another.

On the other hand, the relevant alternative may be even less appealing. Advocates of approval voting point out that simple plurality is conducive to insincere voting in favor of major parties, and they regard approval voting as the easiest fix available. They cite survey evidence that, with approval voting, the vote for independents would at least triple.[21]

4.12 Score Voting (also called "Range Voting" and "the Point System")

4.12.1 How the System Selects the Winner

An election is held to fill one position. An official ballot lists individuals eligible to win the election and perhaps invites a write-in. The ballot tells a voter to assign a rating in a particular range, such as 0 to 10 or 0 to 100, to each of as many of those candidates as the voter wishes. The instructions may add that, if a voter does not assign a rating to a particular candidate, then the blank will be replaced by an average of the ratings received by that candidate from other voters.

Officials determine the arithmetic mean of the of each candidate's ratings, and the winner is whichever candidate has the highest mean (or, perhaps, whichever candidate has the highest mean of, say, three or more non-blank ratings).

4.12.2 Numerical Example

Let us again use the rankings in Table 3. Then six individuals, namely, Abe, Ben, Cal, Dee, Eve, and Fay, are eligible for a vacant seat and 27 persons are eligible to vote.

What appears on the ballots depends on what numbers each voter may and does choose. We will consider three possibilities.

In Case 1, each voter assigns a rating of (a) 100 to the candidate ranked first by that voter, (b) 80 to the candidate ranked second by that voter, (c) 60 to the candidate ranked third by that voter, (d) 40 to the candidate ranked fourth by that voter, (e) 20 to the candidate ranked fifth by that voter, and (f) 0 to the candidate ranked sixth by that voter. Table 22a shows the arithmetic means of the ratings that then are assigned to each candidate, and Table 22d shows which candidate would win the election with those means.

---

[21]See Steven Brams and Peter Fishburn, "Going from theory to practice: the mixed success of Approval Voting," Social Choice and Welfare 25:457–474, 2005, and Brams, Mathematics and Democracy, Princeton University Press, 2008

Table 22a: Ratings Received if Each Voter Assigns Ratings of 100, 80, 60, 40, 20, and 0

	Number of Voters Involved	Abe	Ben	Cal	Dee	Eve	Fay
	6	600	480	120	360	240	0
	1	100	60	20	80	40	0
Precinct 1	3	300	60	120	180	0	240
	1	40	100	20	60	80	0
	4	0	400	80	160	240	320
	1	20	40	100	0	60	80
	3	0	60	300	120	180	240
Precinct 2	1	20	60	40	100	80	0
	1	20	40	0	100	80	60
	1	20	40	0	100	60	80
	1	20	40	60	0	100	80
	1	20	0	60	40	100	80
Precinct 3	1	0	20	60	40	100	80
	1	20	0	80	40	60	100
	1	20	0	40	80	60	100
Total		1200	1400	1100	1460	1480	1460
Total ÷27		44.4	51.9	40.7	54.1	54.8	54.1

In Case 2, each voter assigns a rating of (a) 100 to the candidate ranked first by that voter, (b) 60 (instead of 80) to the candidate ranked second by that voter, (c) 50 (instead of 60) to the candidate ranked third by that voter, (d) 40 to the candidate ranked fourth by that voter, (e) 20 to the candidate ranked fifth by that voter, and (f) 0 to the candidate ranked sixth by that voter. Table 22b shows the arithmetic means of the ratings that then are assigned to each candidate, and Table 22d shows which candidate would win the election with those means.

Table 22b: Ratings Received if Each Voter Assigns Ratings of 100, 60, 50, 40, 20, and 0

	Number of Voters Involved	Abe	Ben	Cal	Dee	Eve	Fay
Precinct 1	6	600	360	120	300	240	0
	1	100	50	20	60	40	0
	3	300	60	120	150	0	180
	1	40	100	20	50	60	0
	4	0	400	80	160	200	240
Precinct 2	1	20	40	100	0	50	60
	3	0	60	300	120	150	180
	1	20	50	40	100	60	0
	1	20	40	0	100	60	50
	1	20	40	0	100	50	60
Precinct 3	1	20	40	50	0	100	60
	1	20	0	50	40	100	60
	1	0	20	50	40	100	60
	1	20	0	60	40	50	100
	1	20	0	40	60	50	100
Total		1200	1260	1050	1320	1310	1150
Total ÷27		44.4	46.7	38.9	48.9	48.5	42.6

In Case 3, each voter assigns a rating of (a) 100 to the candidate ranked first by that voter, (b) 50 (instead of 60) to the candidate ranked second by that voter, (c) 30 (instead of 50) to the candidate ranked third by that voter, (d) 20 (instead of 40) to the candidate ranked fourth by that voter, (e) 10 (instead of 20) to the candidate ranked fifth by that voter, and (f) 0 to the candidate ranked sixth by that voter. Table 22c shows the arithmetic means of the ratings that then are assigned to each candidate, and Table 22d shows which candidate would win the election with those means.

Table 22c: Ratings Received if Each Voter Assigns Ratings of 100, 50, 30, 20, 10, and 0

	Number of Voters Involved	Abe	Ben	Cal	Dee	Eve	Fay
	6	600	300	60	180	120	0
	1	100	30	10	50	20	0
Precinct 1	3	300	30	60	90	0	150
	1	20	100	10	30	50	0
	4	0	400	40	80	120	200
	1	10	20	100	0	30	50
	3	0	30	300	60	90	150
Precinct 2	1	10	30	20	100	50	0
	1	10	20	0	100	50	30
	1	10	20	0	100	30	50
	1	10	20	30	0	100	50
	1	10	0	30	20	100	50
Precinct 3	1	0	10	30	20	100	50
	1	10	0	50	20	30	100
	1	10	0	20	50	30	100
Total		1100	1010	760	900	920	980
Total ÷27		40.7	37.4	28.1	33.3	34.1	36.3

Table 22d consolidates and compares the three cases.

Table 22d: Outcome with Score Voting

	If the Six Ratings Assigned by Each Voter Are:		
	100, 80, 60, 40, 20, 0	100, 60, 50, 40, 20, 0	100, 50, 30, 20, 10, 0
	Then, with Sincere Voting, the Arithmetic-Mean Scores Are:		
Abe	44.4	44.4	40.7
Ben	51.9	46.7	37.4
Cal	40.7	38.9	28.1
Dee	54.1	48.9	33.3
Eve	54.8	48.5	34.1
Fay	54.1	42.6	36.3
Winner	Eve	Dee	Abe

There are three different outcomes. As Table 22d indicates, the winner is Eve in Case 1, Dee in Case 2, and Abe in Case 3. Since there is no objectively correct way to choose a rating, and since different voters may give different meaning to the same difference in ratings, thereby undermining comparability, this variation of outcomes is unnerving.

4.12.3   Who Uses Score Voting

American mathematician Warren D. Smith launched a campaign for Score Voting in 2000.[22] The system is not being used in public elections, but it is widely used for other purposes.

In boxing, gymnastics, figure skating, ballroom dancing, cooking, dressage, and some other scored contests, each judge assigns a rating, and the contestant with the highest average score wins. (In a multi-winner version, two or more contestants — those with the highest averages — win.)

Similarly, some families announce ratings — and even average them — when choosing a restaurant, a pet, a car, a house, etc.

Another user is The Harvey Milk Club, the largest Democratic club in San Francisco. It uses Score Voting for its endorsements, asking a voter to assign 5, 4, 3, 2, 1, or 0 when rating an alternative.

And another user is the German Pirate Party, which on 13-May-2012 received 7.8% of the votes in North Rhine-Westphalia (Germany's largest state). It uses Score Voting to select its chairman and other officers.

---

[22]W. Smith, "Range voting" at http://scorevoting.net/WarrenSmithPages/homepage/rangevote.ps.

4.12.4   Tactics with Score Voting

One reason why many people like Score Voting is that it allows — indeed, requires — a voter to register strength of preference, that is, degree of like or dislike of the alternatives, and that seems appropriate in many contexts. For example, when a family or group of friends is making a choice (for example, choosing a restaurant), indications of strength of preference are likely to be sincere, comparable, welcome, respected, and useful.

However, when there are many voters, secret ballots, and impersonal results, the situation changes. Indications of strength of preference then are likely to be tactical.

In particular, Score Voting invites use of a burying tactic, namely, giving the lowest allowed rating to a candidate whom the voter fears will defeat a candidate that the voter likes more or dislikes less. Conversely, score voting invites giving the highest allowed rating to whichever candidate the voter ranks first. Voters using this approach not only enhance the chances of their favorite but also tend to give their ballot more weight than the ballots of voters who do not exaggerate differences between candidates.

4.12. Score Voting

Chapter 5

Which One-Winner System is Best?

5.1   The Gibbard-Satterthwaite Strategy Theorem

You may want an election system that offers no reward to tactical voting. Unfortunately, unless the winner will be chosen by chance (as with the Coptic pope) and perhaps not even then — no such a system is available. American philosopher Allan Gibbard and American economist Mark Satterthwaite published that conclusion in the 1970s.[1]

The Gibbard-Satterthwaite theorem says that, when there are three or more candidates and three or more voters, one of the following three statements must hold for every voting rule that has universal domain (that is, the rule converts any set of voter preferences into a decision), chooses a single winner, and is deterministic (that is, does not have a random component — for example, electing the top choice on a ballot chosen by chance):

1. The rule is dictatorial, that is, there is a single individual who can choose the winner, or

2. There is some candidate who can never win under the rule, or

3. The rule is susceptible to tactical voting, in the sense that there are conditions under which a voter who knows how other voters will vote can obtain a more-preferred outcome by voting in a manner that does not reflect his or her preferences.

To conclude with Statement 3, simply refuse to adopt any voting rule that satisfies Statements 1 and 2, explaining that they are undemocratic or unfair; that leaves Statement

---

[1]A. Gibbard, "Manipulation of voting schemes: a general result." Econometrica 41 (4): 587'601, 1973. M. Satterthwaite, "Strategy-proofness and Arrow's Conditions: Existence and Correspondence Theorems for Voting Procedures and Social Welfare Functions", Journal of Economic Theory 10,:187'217, 1975.

3 — and the conclusion that no election system that is democratic and rolls no dice will be strategy-proof.

On the other hand, election systems differ in this respect. Tactical voting is easier to plan and implement — and therefore more likely — with some systems than with others. Furthermore, as we have seen, what tactics are effective varies with the system is being used. Accordingly, resistance to strategy, also known as sincere voting, belongs on the list of criteria used to compare and evaluate alternative election systems.

5.2   Independence of Irrelevant Alternatives ("IIA")

There is reason to want an election system to be independent of irrelevant alternatives, in the sense that (warning: there are other definitions) adding or removing a non-winning candidate will not change the winner. An election system satisfying IIA is not vulnerable to a deplorable — but common — tactic, namely, nominating a spoiler, that is, a candidate who splits the opposition's vote and defeats their candidate.

However, IIA is too strong a demand. None of the twelve single-winner systems that we have considered satisfy IIA.

Three of those systems, namely, Majority Judgment, approval voting, and score voting, do not satisfy IIA because disqualifying a non-winning candidate who was a particular voter's top choice may elevate the rating of that voter's second choice — and therefore change the winner.

The other nine systems that we have considered do not satisfy IIA because, if one of three candidates is disqualified, those systems use majority rule to choose between the other two candidates — and electing either of those other two candidates will violate IIA if the disqualified candidate would have defeated the winner.

A numerical example may clarify the point. Suppose that (a) there are three candidates, namely, Abe, Ben, and Cal; and (b) 25% of voters rank Abe >Ben >Cal; 40% rank Ben >Cal >Abe; and 35% rank Cal >Abe >B.

There are three cases to consider.

1. If Abe and Ben are the finalists, then Abe will defeat Ben (by 60% to 40%) — and electing Abe will violate IIA because Cal would defeat Abe (by 75% to 25%) if Abe and Cal but not Ben were candidates.

2. If Ben and Cal are the finalists, then Ben will defeat Cal (by 65% to 35%) — and electing Ben will violate IIA because Abe would defeat Ben (by 60% to 40%) if Abe and Ben but not Cal were candidates.

3. If Abe and Cal are the finalists, then Cal will defeat Abe (by 75% to 25%) — and electing Cal will violate IIA because Ben would defeat Cal (by 65% to 35%) if Ben and Cal but not Abe were candidates.

Since one of Abe, Ben, and Cal in fact will be the winner, the outcome — and therefore the election system — will violate IIA.

So reconcile yourself to having an election system that allows nomination of a spoiler or vote-splitter to alter the outcome of an election.

5.3   May's Theorem

In the three cases just considered, majority rule played a central role, and American mathematician Kenneth May showed why that is reasonable.[2]

May identified four objectives. They are (1) Decisiveness (that is, the system converts any set of voter preferences into a decision, a property later called "Universal Domain"), (2) Neutrality (that is, the system treats voters equally), (3) Anonymity (that is, the system treats candidates equally), and (4) Positive Responsiveness (that is, if any voter elevates his rating or ranking of a candidate who was either a tied winner or the sole winner, then that candidate will become or remain the sole winner).

May showed that, when there are exactly two candidates and an odd number of voters, and more voters prefer one candidate than prefer the other, then an election system will satisfy those four objectives if — and only if — the system chooses whichever of those two candidates is preferred by the larger number of voters.

So do not abandon majority rule casually.

5.4   Nakamura's Theorem

Japanese game theorist Kenjiro Nakamura gave us Nakamura's theorem. It complements both May's theorem and Condorcet's paradox of voting.

May showed that majority rule is able to choose a winner when there are two candidates — and is a reasonable way to do so. Condorcet showed that, with majority rule, every one of three or more candidates may lose a paired comparison with at least one other candidate. Nakamura's theorem generalizes Condorcet's paradox.

Nakamura's theorem obtains a number — it is called "the Nakamura number" — for each single-winner election system. The Nakamura number for a system is an integer, namely, the smallest number of candidates that is not small enough to enable that election system to choose a winner with any possible set of voter preferences.[3]

For majority rule, the Nakamura number is 3. Accordingly, as Condorcet indicated, the largest number of candidates from which majority rule will, with any possible set of voter preferences, choose a winner is two.

---

[2]Kenneth O. May, "A Set of Independent Necessary and Sufficient Conditions for Simple Majority Decision," Econometrica, 20(4): 680'684, 1952.

[3]K. Nakamura, "The Vetoers in a Simple Game with Ordinal Preferences." International Journal of Game Theory 8: 55'61, 1979.

5.5 Arrow's Theorem

In 1950, American economist Kenneth Arrow published an unwelcome conclusion.[4] It and related work produced a Nobel prize for Arrow (shared with John R. Hicks) in 1972. Throughout the world, the conclusion is now known as Arrow's impossibility theorem.

Arrow's theorem has a popular version. As phrased in an MIT publication, the popular version is "Arrow's Theorem Proves No Voting System is Perfect."[5]

This conclusion is both correct and useful. An important example is that no election system can guarantee both (a) Condorcet compliance and (b) Later no harm. "Condorcet compliance" means that, if one of the candidates would receive more than half of the votes cast in a two-candidate runoff regardless of which other candidate was in that runoff, then that candidate will win the election. Many writers regard this rule as fundamental to democracy.

"Later no harm" means that whether and how a voter ranks candidates below a particular candidate will not cause the latter candidate to lose the election.[6] Many writers regard this rule as a prerequisite for sincere voting.

Both criteria are reasonable demands, but they are not compatible. Every election system that fulfills one of these two objectives will fail the other and, at least to that extent, will be imperfect. In short, no election system can have every characteristic that seems democratic and/or internally consistent.

That no election system is perfect, however, is not Arrow's theorem. In fact, Arrow's theorem is not about election systems, that is, procedures for selecting one or more individuals for a specified status based on preferences expressed by members of a specified electorate. Instead, Arrow's theorem is about "social-welfare functions", that is, rules for obtaining a social ranking of three or more candidates from the rankings of those candidates by three or more individual voters.

In particular, as revised by Arrow in 1963, Arrow's theorem concludes that no social-welfare function — note: no social-welfare function — can simultaneously satisfy all of the following six conditions:[7]

1. **Universal Domain:** That is, the rule will transform any conceivable set of rankings of three or more candidates by three or more voters (such as the set Abe >Ben >Cal, Ben >Cal >Abe, and Cal >Abe >Ben) into a single social ranking of those candidates for that group of voters (such as Abe >Ben >Cal).

2. **Connectedness:** That is, if Abe and Ben are candidates, then the social ranking of candidates will indicate either that Abe is as at least as desirable as Ben or that Ben

---

[4]Kenneth J. Arrow, "A Difficulty in the Concept of Social Welfare", Journal of Political Economy 58(4):328'346, 1950. Arrow elaborated in K. J. Arrow, Social Choice and Individual Values., Wiley, 1951.

[5]Massachusetts Institute of Technology, The Tech Online Edition, 123(8), February 28, 2003.

[6]Douglas R. Woodall, "Properties of Preferential Election Rules", Voting matters, 3:8–15, 199

[7]Kenneth J. Arrow, Social Choice and Individual Values, 2nd ed., Yale, 1963.

is as at least as desirable as Abe.

3. **Social Transitivity:** That is, if Abe, Ben, and Cal are candidates and the social ranking of candidates indicates both that Abe is as at least as desirable as Ben and that Ben is at least as desirable as Cal, then the social ranking also will indicate that Abe is at least as desirable as Cal.

4. **Independence of Irrelevant Alternatives:** That is, disqualifying a candidate will not alter the social ranking of other candidates.

5. **Pareto Consistency or Unanimity:** That is, if Abe and Ben are candidates and every voter ranks Abe ahead of Ben, then Abe will rank ahead of Ben in the social ranking.

6. **Nondictatorship:** That is, the preferences of more than one voter determine candidates' social ranking. (Nondictatorship, incidentally, is less demanding than a condition introduced by other writers, namely, Anonymity, that is, equal treatment of all voters.)

Arrow's proof consisted of showing that a social-welfare function that satisfies Conditions 1–5 above will violate Condition 6.

Among scholars, attention focused on Condition 4, that is, on Independence of Irrelevant Alternatives. IIA seemed to be both the least fundamental and least appropriate of the six conditions, and some specialists suggested weakening IIA or dropping it entirely. Supposedly, a social-welfare function then could satisfy Arrow's other five conditions.[8]

However, IIA is not really the problem. The real reason that Conditions 1–6 are incompatible is that (a) Condition 1, that is, Universal Domain, requires that a rule for social ranking transform any conceivable set of three or more rankings of three or more candidates into a social ranking of those candidates, while Condition 3 that is, Social Transitivity, requires that the ranking so obtained be complete and transitive; (b) nothing Arrow mentions forbids using Majority Rule to decide whether Abe socially ranks above, with, or below Ben; and (c) Majority Rule may — as Condorcet's Paradox of Voting and Nakamura's theorem say — be unable to produce the transitive social ranking of pairs of candidates demanded by Conditions 1 and 3.

So let's settle for the popular version of Arrow's theorem. Despite being a misinterpretation, it is both correct and useful. It says that no election system can have all properties that seem democratic and/or internally consistent.

---

[8]See Kenneth J. Arrow, Amartya K. Sen and Kotaro Suzumura, eds., Handbook of Social Choice and Welfare, Elsevier, 2002.

5.6   Table 1 Revisited

Table 1 above listed ten goals for a multi-winner election system. Table 23 shows how each of the twelve single-winner systems discussed in this section performs in each of these ten respects. The entries in the table, except for "Elicits ratings", "Vote once", and "Verifiable", come from the literature of social-choice theory.[9]

Table 23 is disappointing. It indicates that no single-winner election system dominates. That is, for none of the systems does a paired comparison with each of the other systems indicate that that system is more desirable in some respects and no less desirable in the other respects. Hence, even if you agree with the eleven goals listed in the table, you cannot identify a best system unless you compare the advantages and disadvantages of each system, and that is both difficult and subjective.

Suppose you are inclined to take account of the strength of voters' preferences and therefore are inclined to favor a system that asks voters to rate the candidates (as distinct from ranking, approving, or choosing them). Two of the systems reviewed above do that, namely, Score Voting and Majority Judgment. Both systems average the ratings received.

Unfortunately, the numbers that Score Voting averages are suspect. A shrewd voter is likely to give (a) the lowest allowed rating to every candidate whom the voter fears will defeat a candidate that the voter likes more (or dislikes less), and (b) the highest allowed rating to the voter's most-preferred candidate and, if the latter is a long shot, also to the most-preferred of the candidates who seem to have a chance to win. Furthermore, although voters' intermediate ratings can determine which candidate wins — remember how changing the numerical value of voters' intermediate ratings changed the winner from Eve to Dee and then to Abe — those ratings are chosen arbitrarily and may not be comparable.

Different voters' ratings are likely to be more comparable with Majority Judgment than with Score Voting. Limiting the number of ratings to about six and using ratings such as "Good" and "Fair", which tend to have the same meaning for different voters, enhances comparability. Also, referring to the median rating, rather than to the arithmetic mean of ratings, equalizes the impact of all one-step changes in a candidate's ratings. On the other hand, with Majority Judgment, as with Score Voting, a shrewd voter is likely to give the lowest allowed rating to a candidate whom the voter fears will defeat a candidate that the voter likes more (or dislikes less) and to give the highest allowed rating to whichever candidate the voter most prefers.

Because Score Voting and Majority Judgment have these deficiencies, or perhaps because neither of them is Condorcet compliant, you may want to consider some other systems.

If so, you should consider a system that discourages tactical voting and that, with sincere voting, will elect a pairwise champion whenever there is one. Two of the systems

---

[9]See, for example, Nicolaus Tideman, Collective Decisions and Voting, Ashgate, 2006, pp. 165–244.

Table 23: Merits and Demerits of the Twelve Single-Winner Election Systems Reviewed Above

	Simple Plurality	Runoff	Exhaustive	Full IRV	Coombs	Borda	Bucklin	Majority Judgement	Schulze	Maximin	Approval	Score
Elicits Ratings[1]	No	No	No	No	No	No	No	Yes	No	No	No	Yes
Condorcet Efficiency[2]	0.61	0.81	0.88	0.88	0.88(?)	0.87	0.90(?)	0.90(?)	1	1	0.68	0.80(?)
Mutual Majority[3]	No	No	No	Yes	No	No	Yes	Yes	Yes	No	Yes	Yes
Monotonic[4]	Yes	No	No	No	No	Yes	Yes	Yes	Yes	Yes	Yes	Yes
Later No Harm[5]	–	–	–	Yes	No	No	No	No	No	No	No	No
Independent of Clones[6]	No	No	Yes	Yes	No	No	No	Yes	Yes	No	Yes	Yes
Sincere Voting[7]	63 (Fair)	81 (Good)	97 (Fine)	97 (Fine)	43 (Poor)	46 (Poor)	58 (Fair)	40 (Poor)	89 (Fine)	89 (Fine)	39 (Poor)	40 (Poor)
Transparent[8]	100 (Fine)	90 (Good)	80 (Fair)	80 (Fair)	70 (Fair)	90 (Good)	80 (Fair)	90 (Good)	40 (Poor)	70 (Fair)	90 (Good)	90 (Good)
Vote Once[9]	Yes	No	No	Yes	Yes	Yes	Yes	Yes	Yes	Yes	Yes	Yes
Verifiable[10]	Yes	Yes	Yes	No	No	Yes	Yes	No	No	No	Yes	No

[1] Voters indicate the strength of their preferences.
[2] The probability that, when one of the candidates would receive more than half of the votes cast in a two-candidate runoff against each of the other candidates, that candidate will in fact be elected.
[3] If there is a subset of the candidates such that more than half of the voters strictly prefer every member of the subset to every candidate outside the subset, then the winner will come from the subset.
[4] Elevating the rank that a voter assigns to a particular candidate, while making no change in the order of other candidates, will not deprive that candidate of victory.
[5] Whether and how a voter ranks candidates below a particular candidate will not cause the latter candidate to lose the election.
[6] Suppose that two candidates are so alike that no voter would rank any other candidate between them. Then, if each of the two would be elected provided the other were not a candidate, one of the two will be elected if both are candidates. And, if each would lose provided the other were not a candidate, then each will lose if the other is a candidate.
[7] It is likely that voters will report their true preferences.
[8] It is easy for voters to understand how the outcome will be determined.
[9] The outcome will be determined with a single round of voting.
[10] The outcome can be confirmed simply by re-tallying ballots and re-adding subtotals.

reviewed above have these characteristics, namely the Schulze system and the Maximin system. Both use a ballot that asks a voter to rank the candidates or, rather, to rank as many of the candidates as the voter wishes.

Compared to Maximin, Schulze has the advantage of being mutual-majority compliant and independent of clones. On the other hand, because Schulze's rule for Condorcet completion is virtually unintelligible, Maximin has the advantage of being more transparent and more verifiable.

For Nicolaus Tideman, America's leading election theorist, Maximin's advantage in transparency is sufficient to tip the balance. He suggests using Maximin until the public is ready for a more complicated member of the family of Condorcet-compliant systems, such as the Schulze system or Tideman's own ranked-pairs system.[10]

If you favor Condorcet compliance but think that even the Maximin system is too lacking in transparency and verifiability, then consider the Bucklin system. It chose the Condorcet alternative, that is, candidate Fay, in our numerical example, and it seems to have relatively high Condorcet efficiency. The system tends to choose the Condorcet alternative when one is available because — unlike instant-runoff voting — it takes voters' second choices into account, thereby selecting a centrist when few voters have the same first choice but many have the same second choice. It is also easier with Bucklin than with IRV to verify that there was no mistake and no fraud.

We discussed several other systems that use a ranking ballot, namely, Exhaustive Voting, Repeated Voting, the Borda system, and the Coombs system. Exhaustive and repeated have the merit of allowing voters to reconsider and change their rankings, but those systems require that voters assemble in one place. Borda has good transparency, but it uses arbitrary weights to convert ranks to points, Also, Borda fails mutual-majority compliance, later no harm, no spoilers, independence of clones, and sincere voting. In addition to failing those criteria, Coombs also fails monotonicity — though Coombs does have good Condorcet efficiency .

You may like the Bucklin system or some other system that uses a ranking ballot but think that the electorate will reject or misuse such a ballot or that obtaining equipment that can process such a ballot would be inordinately expensive. If so, consider the Top-2 version of runoff voting. Like simple plurality (that is, first-past-the-post), runoff voting uses a choose-one ballot, but it is much more Condorcet efficient and much more conducive to sincere voting than simple plurality. To minimize re-voting (which entails delayed resolution, turnover of voters, and added public and private expense), the rules can provide for waiving the second round of voting if (as in Argentina) the front-runner receives either at least 45% or at least 40% and a 10-point lead.

Another way to replace simple plurality without introducing a ranking ballot is to adopt approval voting. It assures that there will be merely one round of voting. With approval voting, however, expect tactical voting. A shrewd voter will withhold approval of

---

[10]N. Tideman, Collective Decisions and Voting, Ashgate, 2006. p. 242.

an acceptable candidate whom the voter fears will defeat a candidate that the voter likes even more, and also will give approval to a candidate whom the voter dislikes (along with all candidates that the voter ranks higher) in order to defeat a candidate whom the voter dislikes even more and fears will be elected. Nevertheless, unlike simple plurality, Approval does not force a voter to choose between (a) helping a candidate whom the voter dislikes (for example, George W. Bush) to win by the wasting a vote on a loser (for example, Ralph Nader), and (b) helping the voter's second choice (for example, Al Gore), who happens to be the pairwise champion, to win.

Since no single-winner system is dominant, there is no demonstrably correct answer to the title question, that is, which election system is best. Each of us must supply our own answer.

Part II

Ten Multi-Winner Election Systems

Chapter 6

How The Systems Differ

The multi-winner election systems that we will consider differ in two respects. First, the systems elicit information about voters' preferences differently. Seven different ballots are used, as follows:

1. One system invites a voter to choose as many candidates as there are openings.

2. Another system invites a voter to choose a number of candidates but sets that number below the number of openings.

3. Another system gives a voter as many votes as there are openings and invites the voter to distribute those votes among the candidates.

4. Three systems invite a voter to rank two or more candidates in order of preference.

5. One system tells a voter to choose a political party.

6. Another system tells a voter to indicate a preference either for a party or both for a party and for individuals on the party's list of candidates.

7. Two systems tell a voter to choose both a national political party and one or more local representatives.

Second, the systems determine the winners differently. Again there are seven different rules:

1. Three systems award seats to whichever candidates receive the most votes.

2. Two systems sequentially eliminate and elect candidates and then transfer votes from them to other candidates

3. Another system sequentially eliminates and elects candidates and transfers votes from them to other candidates but adds constraints on the outcome (for example, at least one winner must be female).

4. One system awards seats to political parties in proportion to the votes that each party receives — but only to parties that receive more than, say, 5% of the votes cast.

5. One system simultaneously determines how many seats a party wins and which individuals on the party's list receive those seats.

6. Another system simultaneously awards seats in a national legislature both to national political parties and to individual district-representatives.

7. Another system simultaneously awards seats in a national legislature both to national political parties and to individual district-representatives — but awards seats to a party only to compensate for disproportionality in the district results.

Chapter 7

Illustrative Initial Conditions

To illustrate how each system works — and also to compare the outcomes — we will see which candidates each system would elect in a particular case. In that case, which is hypothetical, there are nine candidates (namely, Abe, Ben, Cal, Dee, Eve, Fay, Gil, Hal, and Ian), three polling stations, and 100 voters, and the voters rank the candidates as indicated in Table 24.

Table 24: Rankings Used Below

Rankings of Candidates	Number of Voters with that Ranking:
Abe >Ben >Cal	13
Ben >Abe >Cal	12
Cal >Abe >Ben	10
Dee >Eve >Fay	17
Eve >Dee >Fay	16
Gil >Hal >Ian	32

Using this scenario, we will again see that changing the election system changes the outcome.

Chapter 8

The Ten Systems

8.1 Multi-Winner Plurality (also known as "multi-vote plurality", "At-Large Plurality", "Bloc Voting", and "Vote-for-up-to-n")

8.1.1 How the System Selects the Winners

An election is held to fill two or more positions in a legislative chamber. An official ballot states how many seats are open, invites each voter to choose up to that number of candidates, lists individuals eligible to win a seat, and perhaps invites write-ins.

For each valid ballot on which a qualified candidate is chosen, that candidate receives one "vote" (except that, when directors of a business corporation are being elected, being chosen by a voter confers one vote for each voting share held by that voter).

When n positions are open, the n candidates who receive the most votes are elected (except that, in the case of some business corporations, a candidate must also receive majority support). Ties are broken by lot.

8.1.2 Numerical Example

With the raw data in Table 24, nine candidates are eligible for three vacant seats, and 100 persons are eligible to vote. Suppose that all persons eligible to vote submit a valid ballot, choose three candidates, and vote sincerely — which, with multi-winner plurality, means both that a voter who chooses a particular candidate also chooses every candidate whom that voter ranks above the chosen candidate, and that a voter who does not choose a particular candidate also does not choose any candidate whom that voter ranks below the unchosen candidate. Table 25a shows the result.

Table 25a: Likely Outcome with Multi-Winner Plurality

	Number of Votes If All Voters Choose Their 3 Most-Preferred Candidates
Abe	35
Ben	35
Cal	35
Dee	33
Eve	33
Fay	33
Gil	32
Hal	32
Ian	32
Total	300
Winners	Abe, Ben, Cal

8.1.3 Who Uses Multi-Winner Plurality

Multi-winner plurality is used in city, county, and district elections throughout England, Wales, and the United States. For example, it is used in electing Maryland's House of Delegates and the city council of many California cities

Multi-winner plurality also is used in electing part or all of a dozen national legislatures. That occurs in Cayman Islands, Falkland Islands, Guernsey, Kuwait, Laos, Lebanon, Maldives, Mauritius, Palestine, Syria, Tonga, and Tuvalu.

8.1.4 Proportionality

Table 25a contains a very disproportionate outcome. Voters whose top three choices are Abe, Ben, and Cal constitute 35% of the electorate, but candidates favored by that 35% and disfavored by all other voters win 100% of the open seats. It is reasonable to characterize this result as almost the worst possible outcome — and also to guess that it is what is most likely to occur.

Michael Gallagher, an Irish political scientist, proposed a measure of disproportionality.[1] Its value is 0 if the proportion of open seats won by each party's candidates is the

---

[1]See M. Gallagher, "Proportionality, Disproportionality and Electoral Systems", Electoral Studies 10:3'51, 1991, and M. Gallagher and P. Mitchell, eds., The Politics of Electoral Systems. Oxford University Press, 2005.

same as that party's proportion of the votes received. Conversely, the index equals 1 if a party receiving 100% of the votes wins none of the open seats while a party receiving no votes wins all of the open seats.

With multi-winner plurality, voters vote for individuals, not parties. Nevertheless, if we divide voters into factions, we can use a version of Gallagher's index. Since three seats are open in our example, it seems reasonable to divide our voters into groups whose three top candidates are, in any order, the same, namely, (a) "Faction ABC", consisting of the 35 voters whose top three candidates are a permutation of Abe, Ben, and Cal; (b) "Faction DEF", consisting of the 33 voters whose top three candidates are a permutation of Dee, Eve, and Fay; and (c) "Faction GHI", consisting of the 32 voters whose top three candidates are Gil, Hal, and Ian. With these three factions, the value of the index is 0.563, obtained as follows here S is the proportion of seats received and V is the proportion of votes received:

$$
\begin{aligned}
I_D &= \sqrt{\frac{1}{2} \cdot \sum_{factions} (S - V)^2} \\
&= \sqrt{\frac{1}{2} \cdot \left((1 - 0.35)^2 + (0 - 0.33)^2 + (0 - 0.32)^2 \right)} \\
&= \sqrt{\frac{1}{2} \cdot \left(0.65^2 + -0.33^2 + -0.32^2 \right)} \\
&= \sqrt{\frac{1}{2} \cdot (0.4225 + 0.1089 + 0.1024)} \\
&= \sqrt{.5 \cdot 0.6338} \\
&= \sqrt{0.3169} \\
&= 0.5629
\end{aligned}
$$

Below, we will compare this value with several others.

8.1.5 Tactical Voting with multi-winner plurality

Multi-winner plurality invites a tactic called "bullet voting." This involves choosing only one candidate even though the voter is not indifferent about candidates other than the one chosen. Bullet-voters think it is more important to help their first choice beat their second choice than to help their second choice beat their third and lower choices. Similarly, voters may choose merely two candidates, thinking that it is more important to help their second choice beat their third choice than to help their third choice beat their fourth and lower choices.

Bullet voting may or may not work. Case 2 in Table 25b shows that, if all voters choose only their most-preferred candidate, then the winners are Dee, Eve, and Gil. Compared to the outcome in Table 25a, where all voters chose their top three and the winners were Abe,

Ben, and Cal, this outcome is much better for Faction DEF and Faction GHI but much worse for Faction ABC. Similarly, Case 5 in Table 25b shows that choosing two candidates instead of three would have made the outcome worse for Faction ABC. For Faction ABC, choosing either one or two candidates instead of three deprives their second and third choices of the support needed to defeat, not their first choice, but rather their fourth and lower choices.

Table 25b: Other Outcomes with Multi-Winner Plurality

| | Votes | | | |
	Case 2	Case 3	Case 4	Case 5
Abe	13	23	13	35
Ben	12	12	12	25
Cal	10	0	10	10
Dee	17	17	33	33
Eve	16	16	0	33
Fay	0	0	0	0
Gil	32	32	32	32
Hal	0	0	0	32
Ian	0	0	0	0
Total	100	100	100	200
Winners	Dee, Eve, Gil	Abe, Dee, Gil	Abe, Dee, Gil	Abe, Dee, Eve
I_D for 3 Factions	0.3435	0.0153	0.0153	0.3287

Case 2: All voters choose their one most-preferred candidate.

Case 3: All voters choose their one most-preferred candidate except that 10 voters choose Abe instead of Cal.

Case 4: All voters choose their one most-preferred candidate except that 16 voters choose Dee instead of Eve.

Case 5: All voters choose their two most-preferred candidates.

Nevertheless, bullet voting is not unusual. For example, the city council of Davis, California, is elected by multi-winner plurality, and 29% of the ballots submitted in the last seven two-seat elections cast only one vote.

Another tactic used with multi-winner plurality is compromising. That involves choosing a candidate that the voter ranks below a candidate not chosen by that voter in the hope that the chosen candidate will be elected instead of a candidate ranked even lower.

Like bullet voting, compromising may or may not work. Table 25b shows that, if ten bullet voters choose Abe (their second choice) instead of Cal (their first choice), then the winners change from Dee, Eve, and Gil in Case 2 to Abe, Dee, and Gil in Case 3, successfully giving those ten voters their second choice. On the other hand, Table 25b also shows that that, if 16 bullet voters choose Dee (their second choice) instead of Eve (their first choice), then the winners change from Dee, Eve, and Gil in Case 2 to Abe, Dee, and Gil in Case 4, a worse outcome for those 16 voters.

As American political scientist Gary Cox has explained, accurate information and careful coordination are needed to make tactical voting work.[2]

8.1.6 The California Voting Rights Act

Multi-winner Plurality is under attack in California. California's Voting Rights Act of 2001 says, "An at-large method of election may not be imposed or applied in a manner that impairs the ability of a protected class to elect candidates of its choice ... "[3]. Accordingly, any local council or board in California that is chosen — either partly or entirely — by voters throughout a jurisdiction is vulnerable if there is "racially-polarized voting" in the jurisdiction, that is, a difference between which candidates are preferred by voters in a protected class and which candidates are preferred by the rest of the electorate.

The CVRA is enforced, not by a governmental agency, but rather by private lawsuits; and the act creates a strong financial incentive, not only for interested parties to sue, but also for local governments to anticipate litigation and to acquiesce when it materializes. A local government that loses — or even settles — a CVRA lawsuit, must pay the plaintiff's costs, including legal and court fees.

So far, every plaintiff has demanded changing from a single election district with multiple representatives (usually five) chosen by multi-winner plurality to multiple election districts, each with one representative chosen by simple plurality. And, to date, the plaintiffs have won every case.

In 2003, the Hanford School District agreed to switch to district voting — and paid $110,000 in plaintiff's legal fees as a part of the settlement. The population of the district was 38% Latino, but it had not had a Latino on its board of trustees in 20 years.[4]

In 2008, the Madera School District lost in court. Of the district's students, 82% were Latino, but only one of seven trustees was Latino. An appellate court reduced the attorney's fees that the district was required to pay from $1.7 million to $162,500.[5]

In 2009, the City of Modesto, CA settled — and paid $3.1 million to plaintiff's lawyers and $1.7 million to its own. Over 25% of the city's population was Latino, but the city council had had only one Latino member since 1911.[6]

---

[2]See G. W. Cox, Making Votes Count: Strategic Coordination in the World's Electoral Systems, Cambridge University Press, 1997

[3]California Elections Code. Section 14027.

[4]Gomez v. Hanford JUHSD, Kings County Superior Ct. Case No. 04C0294 (2004). The case never went to trial.

[5]Rey v. Madera Unified School District, 203 Cal.App.4th 1223, 138 Cal. Rptr. 3d (2012).

[6]Sanchez v. City of Modesto, 145 Cal.App.4th 660, 51 Cal.Rptr.3d 821 (2006).

In light of these cases, school districts in Ceres, Esparto, Gustine, and Turlock have agreed to change from at-large to trustee-area elections. Tulare, Escondido, and San Mateo County, which also are being sued, soon may yield, and cities worried about being sued, such as Woodland, CA, also will soon elect their city councils by and from districts.

Santa Clarita, a city of 180,000 in Southern California, is an exception. In March 2014, the plaintiffs offered to settle their CVRA case if the city agreed to use cumulative voting in electing the city council, and the city agreed to do so provided modifying its state-certified equipment would cost less than \$400,000. In addition, the city will pay plaintiff's attorney's fees, but settling quickly held those fees to about \$500,000.[7]

It may be coincidental that groups supporting California's dominant political party have received both the additional seats and plaintiff's fees.

8.1.7   The Federal Voting Rights Act

Multi-winner plurality also is being attacked under the Federal Voting Rights Act of 1965. Implementing the 15th Amendment, Section 2 of the Voting Rights Act says that the states may not impose any "voting qualification or prerequisite to voting, or standard, practice, or procedure . . . to deny or abridge the right of any citizen of the United States to vote on account of race or color."[8] A 1982 amendment adds that discriminatory results are forbidden whether or not there was intent to discriminate.

The VRA is enforced by litigation in a federal district court. Both the U.S. Department of Justice and private plaintiffs have standing, and both have alleged that multi-winner plurality disenfranchises minority voters, partly because minorities are under-registered and partly because peoples' ethnicity determines how they vote.

For a remedy, some complainants have obtained single-member districts and some have obtained a different kind of multi-winner system. The latter has been either limited voting or cumulative voting — but not, oddly, an election system that was designed to produce proportionality for minorities, namely, the single transferable vote.

We turn next to those three systems, that is, to limited voting, cumulative voting, and the single transferable vote.

8.2   Limited Voting (also known as "Partial Bloc Voting")

8.2.1   How the System Selects the Winners

An election is held to fill two or more positions in a legislative chamber. An official ballot (a) lists individuals eligible to win a position, perhaps inviting write-ins, (b) states

---

[7]http://scvnews.com/2014/03/12/city-settles-lawsuit-voting-method-to-change/

[8]42 U.S. C. Sec. 1973. The 15th Amendment says, "The right of citizens of the United States to vote shall not be denied or abridged by the United States or by any State on account of race, color, or previous condition of servitude."

how many candidates a voter may choose (by the definition of "limited voting", this number always is less than the number of open positions), and (c) invites each voter to choose up to that many candidates.

For each valid ballot on which a candidate is chosen, the candidate receives one "vote." When n positions are open, the n candidates receiving the most votes are elected. Officials break a tie, if one occurs, by lot.

8.2.2   Numerical Example

With the raw data in Table 24, nine candidates vie for three vacant seats and 100 persons are eligible to vote. Suppose that every person eligible to vote does vote and that (as in Pennsylvania) a voter may choose up to two candidates. Table 26 shows two likely outcomes.

Table 26: Likely Outcome with Choose-Up-To-Two Limited Voting

| | Votes | |
	Case 1	Case 2
Abe	13	35
Ben	12	25
Cal	10	10
Dee	17	33
Eve	16	33
Fay	0	0
Gil	32	32
Hal	0	32
Ian	0	0
Total	100	200
Winners	Dee, Eve, Gil	Abe, Dee, Eve
I_D for 3 Factions	0.3435	0.3287

Case 1: All voters choose their one most-preferred candidate.
Case 2: All voters choose their two most-preferred candidates.

With multi-winner plurality, in contrast, the winners might be, not only either (a) Dee, Eve, and Gil or (b) Abe, Dee, and Eve, but also either (c) Abe, Ben, and Cal or (d) Abe, Dee, and Gil (see Tables 25a and 25b, above) — and therefore disproportionality, as measured by our index, might be either greater or less.

8.2.3 Who Uses Limited Voting

In some jurisdictions, a voter may vote for only one candidate (this version of limited voting is called "the Single Nontransferable Vote", abbreviated SNTV). SNTV is used to elect the national legislatures of Afghanistan, Indonesia, Jordan, Puerto Rico, Taiwan, Thailand, and Vanuatu. Japan used SNTV to elect its "lower" house (the Shuglin or House of Representatives) from 1948 to 1983 and still uses SNTV to elect its "upper" house (the Sangiin or House of Councillors).

Multi-vote versions of limited voting are used in Gibraltar (10 votes per voter for 17 seats) and Spain (3 votes for your province's four seats in the Senate).

Pennsylvania, too, uses multi-vote versions. Most Pennsylvania counties without a home-rule charter elect three county commissioners with two votes per voter. Also, since 1951, Philadelphia, PA has elected ten members of its city council by district and seven others at-large, and a voter can vote for up to five of the at-large seven (a rule that always yields five Democrat and two Republican winners). The goal is to facilitate multi-party representation.

(Other jurisdictions promote multi-party representation in other ways. Argentina and Mexico use a system intended to produce same result as limited voting with two votes per voter for three seats; specifically, in filling all seats in Argentina's Senate and 96 of 128 seats in Mexico's Senate, two of a constituency's three seats are assigned to the leading party-list and the third seat goes to the runner-up. And Connecticut's General Statutes say that a single political party may not hold more than ⅔ of the seats in a city council, rounded up for councils with fewer than eight members.)

Recently, however, limited voting has been adopted in the U.S., not to promote multi-party representation, but rather as a remedy in civil-rights cases. In these cases, the U.S. Department of Justice alleged that, in violation of Section 2 of the Voting Rights Act of 1965, use of multi-winner plurality was preventing black or Hispanic candidates from being elected to a city council, school board, or county commission. Since 1987, adoption of limited voting has resolved about 30 such cases in five different states (Alabama, Arizona, Georgia, North Carolina, and Ohio).[9]

Different versions of limited voting have been adopted. In 1997, Cleveland County, North Carolina, changed from electing a five-member governing board by multi-winner plurality to filling seven seats with four votes per voter. On the other hand, since 2009, Calera, Alabama, has filled six council seats with one vote per voter. Most often, five-seven seats are filled with 1 or 2 votes per voter.

---

[9]For a summary of cases initiated by the U. S. Department of Justice, see `http://www.justice.gov/crt/about/vot/litigation/recent_sec2.php#ncarolina`

8.2.4   Proportionality

In our initial numerical example of multi-winner plurality (Table 25a, above), candidates favored by Faction ABC and disfavored by other voters won all three open seats even though that faction submitted merely 35% of the valid ballots. Limited voting is supposed to prevent such a disproportionate result, and it did so in our numerical examples (Table 26). However, because candidates favored by Faction DEF, which cast merely 33% of the votes, then filled two of the three open seats, the outcome was still very disproportional.

When different versions of limited voting are compared, it is sometimes said that the opportunity for a minority to elect its favorite candidate is maximized with SNTV, that is, if a voter may not choose more than one party or candidate.[10] While that may be true in other situations, a comparison of Case 1 and Case 2 in Table 26, above, indicates that, with our raw data, disproportionality would be a little greater with SNTV than with choose-up-to-two. More important, in both Case 1 and Case 2, none of the candidates favored by a faction casting about ⅓ of the votes was elected.

Also noteworthy is whether a faction casting a majority of the votes will fill a majority of the open seats. For that, limited voting can be an obstacle. To obtain a share of the winners proportional to its share of the votes cast, a majority faction must identify an appropriate number of candidates and arrange to divide its votes about evenly among those candidates, which is not an easy task.

8.3   Cumulative Voting (also known as "Accumulation Voting" and "Weighted Voting")

8.3.1   How the System Selects the Winners

An election is held to fill two or more positions. An official ballot lists individuals eligible to win those positions, perhaps invites write-in candidates, and states how many votes the voter receiving that ballot may cast.

In a political election with n seats open, each voter may cast n votes. In a corporate election with n directorships open, a voter holding s voting shares may cast $s \cdot n$ votes. In either case, whichever n candidates receive the most votes are elected, and a tie, if one occurs, is broken by lot.

How are votes allocated to candidates? With an "equal-and-even-ballot", a voter's votes are automatically divided evenly among whichever candidates that voter chooses. Alternatively, with a "points-ballot", the ballot tells a voter to mark or write a desired number of votes — or to pull a desired number of levers — next to each candidate's name.

---

[10]See, for example, A. Lipjhart, R. Pintor, and Y. Sone, "The Limited Vote," in B. Grofman and A. Lijphart, eds., Electoral Laws and Their Political Consequences, New York, Agathon Press, 1986, p. 168.

8.3.2 Numerical Example

With the data in Table 24, nine candidates vie for three vacant seats and 100 persons are eligible to vote. Suppose that the ballot tells a voter to distribute three votes among the candidates in whatever way the voter wishes and that all of the 100 voters submit a valid ballot, distributing their votes as shown in Table 27.

Table 27: Outcomes with Cumulative Voting

	Votes		
	Case 1	Case 2	Case 3
Abe	39	48	35
Ben	36	37	35
Cal	30	20	35
Dee	51	50	33
Eve	48	49	33
Fay	0	0	33
Gil	96	64	32
Hal	0	32	32
Ian	0	0	32
Total	300	300	300
Winners	Dee, Eve, Gil	Dee, Eve, Gil	Abe, Ben, Cal
I_D for 3 Factions	0.3435	0.3435	0.5629

Case 1: All voters give 3 votes their first choice.
Case 2: All voters give 2 votes their first choice and 1 vote to their second choice.
Case 3: All voters give 1 vote to each of their first, second and third choices.

8.3.3 Who Uses Cumulative Voting

Cumulative voting was used to elect school boards in England from 1870 to 1902 and to elect the Illinois House of Representatives from 1870 to 1980. In Illinois, each district elected three representatives, and each voter could cast three votes.

A constrained version currently is used in elections for the nine-member assembly of Norfolk Island (an Australian territory dating from 1856, when descendants of the Bounty Mutineers moved there from Pitcairn Island). Norfolk voters cannot give all their votes to one candidate.

In the U.S., many states allow corporate directors to be elected with cumulative voting. Indeed, some states (including California) require it for unlisted corporations.

For public entities, however, cumulative voting, like limited voting, has been adopted in the U.S. primarily as a remedy in voting-rights cases. Since 1987, switching to cumulative voting has resolved about 60 cases pertaining to city councils, county commissions, and school boards in six different states (Alabama, Illinois, New Mexico, New York, South Dakota, and Texas). In addition, many school districts, especially in Texas, have adopted cumulative voting voluntarily.

Both types of ballot are being used. In 1987, Alamogordo, NM, replaced a seven member at-large city council with four single-member districts and three at-large seats to be elected every four years by cumulative voting with a points-ballot. To give all three votes to one candidate, a voter pulls all three levers above that name. In contrast, every four years since 1991, an equal-and-even-ballot has been used to elect half of the ten member city council in Peoria, IL. A voter can cast 5 votes for one candidate, 2½ votes for each of two candidates, 1⅔ votes for each of three candidates, 1¼ votes for each of four candidates, or 1 vote each for each of five candidates. As with limited voting, diversity resulted in more than one sense.

8.3.4 Proportionality

Cumulative voting is supposed to enable a substantial minority of the electorate to win a substantial minority of the open seats. For this proportionality to occur, however, each faction of voters must give all of its votes to a limited number of candidates and, when a faction has enough votes to elect two or more candidates, must give approximately the same number of votes to each of that many candidates.

How many candidates does employing that strategy enable a faction of voters to elect? If n seats are open and a faction casting proportion p of the total number of votes cast wastes none of its votes, then the number of candidates that that faction certainly can elect equals $[p \cdot (n + 1)] - 1$, rounded up to the next higher integer when not itself an integer. For example, if three seats are open and a faction casting 35% of the votes wastes no votes, then the number of candidates that that faction can be sure to elect is $[0.35 \cdot (3 + 1)] - 1 = 0.4$, rounded up to 1.

Conversely, if n seats are open and a total of v votes will be cast, then a faction wanting to be sure to elect a particular candidate must give that candidate at least $\frac{v}{n+1} + 1$ votes, rounded down to the next lower integer when not itself an integer. For example, if three seats are open and a total of 300 votes will be cast, then a faction wanting to be sure to elect a particular candidate must give that candidate at least $\frac{300}{3+1} + 1 = 76$ votes (not rounded because $\frac{300}{3+1} + 1$ itself is an integer). Note that 75 votes would not be enough because three other candidates might also receive 75 votes.

In Case 1 and Case 2 of our numerical example (Table 27), Abe, Ben, and Cal won no seats even though they were the top three choices of 35% of the voters. One of those three candidates certainly would have been elected if those voters had given at least 76 of their 105 votes to that candidate. To accomplish that, however, the 35% needed to choose one of Abe, Ben, and Cal and agree to give that candidate at least 76 votes — and then actually do so.

8.4 Single Transferable Vote (also called "STV", "the Hare-Clark System", and "Choice Voting")

8.4.1 How the System Selects the Winners

An election is held to fill two or more positions in a legislative chamber. An official ballot states how many positions are open, lists individuals eligible to win a position, perhaps invites write-ins, and invites each voter to rank the candidates in order of preference, perhaps by assigning the number 1 to the candidate they most prefer, 2 to their second choice, 3 to their third choice, etc. Usually the candidates are listed alphabetically, perhaps after being grouped by party.

Voters' rankings are converted to seats won in a way intended to make the proportion of seats won by the favorites of each faction of voters as close to the proportion of votes cast by that faction as is possible when neither seats nor winners come in fractions. Seats are filled one at a time, and the process of filling them can be divided into eight steps, as follows.

Step 1: Determine how many votes a candidate must receive in order to win the first seat that is filled. The answer involves a number called the "quota" (or, occasionally, the "threshold").

In its most sophisticated version, the quota is the largest number of votes that is not quite large enough to elect a candidate. Specifically, when the number of open seats is n, the quota equals

$$\frac{1}{n+1} \cdot B \cdot 1\frac{\text{vote}}{\text{ballot}}$$

where B is the number of valid ballots. For example, if three seats are open and 100 ballots are valid, then the quota is $\frac{1}{3+1} \cdot 100 \cdot 1 = 25$. Note that, if exactly 25 votes were sufficient — instead of not quite enough — for election, then four candidates might win the three seats.

After one seat is filled (or, because no candidate has a quota of votes, the candidate with the fewest votes is eliminated from contention), some ballots may be "exhausted." An exhausted ballot is one that no longer ranks at least one continuing candidate, that is, at least one candidate who has neither been elected

©2014 — 108

nor eliminated. If and when at least one ballot is exhausted, it is appropriate to reduce the quota to

$$\frac{1}{1+U} \cdot B$$

where U is the initial total number of unfilled seats and B is the number of valid ballots that have not been exhausted.

Step 2: Determine how many votes each candidate received. A candidate receives one vote for every valid ballot on which that candidate is top choice.

Step 3: See whether at least one candidate has more than a quota of votes and, if so, declare the one with the most votes is elected.

Step 4: Transfer surplus votes, that is, votes in excess of the quota, from the elected candidate to the next choices — better said, to the next not-yet-defeated choices — of the voters for whom that elected candidate was top choice.

Step 5: See whether at least one other candidate has either exactly a quota or more than a quota of votes and, if so, declare the one with the most votes to be elected. Also, again transfer surplus votes from the elected candidate to the next not-yet-defeated choices of the voters for whom that elected candidate was top choice. If all seats have been filled, stop; the election is complete.

Step 6: If not all seats have yet been filled, then declare defeated whichever of the remaining candidates has the fewest votes.

Step 7: Transfer all votes held by the newly-defeated candidate to the next choices — better said, to the next not-yet-defeated choices — of the voters who cast those votes.

Step 8: Repeat this process of election, transfer of surplus, elimination, and transfer of votes until all seats have been filled. At that point, each faction of voters will have obtained representatives approximately in proportion to that faction's proportion of the electorate.

Steps 4 and 7 are what produces proportionality. Step 4, that is, transferring surplus votes from a newly-elected candidate to supporters' next choices, assures that a faction of voters is not denied its share of representatives merely because members of the faction named fewer candidates as top choice than the faction had enough votes to elect. With surplus transferred, a faction's votes are distributed among candidates as the faction would choose if it were one person and knew how other factions were voting.

When STV was first used (in Denmark in 1857), surplus moved physically. For each contest, officials sorted ballots by top choice, put all ballots with the same top choice into a pile for that candidate, determined which candidates had enough votes to be elected on the first tally, determined how many of a winner's votes were surplus, randomly removed that many ballots from the winner's pile, identified the next choices on those removed ballots, and put the removed ballots on the piles of the candidates ranked next on those ballots. A candidate had as many votes as there were ballots in his pile.

In sophisticated contemporary versions of STV, surplus votes are not transferred that way. Surplus votes go, not to the next choices on a random selection of the ballots that caused the newly-elected candidate to be elected, but to the next choices on all ballots giving votes to the newly-elected candidate. Each transferee then receives a fraction of each surplus vote. The fraction equals the newly-elected candidate's surplus votes divided by the newly-elected candidate's total votes.

Similarly, Step 7, that is, transferring votes from a newly-defeated candidate to supporters' next choices, assures that no faction of voters is denied its share of representatives merely because members of the faction named more candidates as top choice than the faction had enough votes to elect. When votes are transferred from a newly-defeated candidate, as when above-quota votes are transferred from a newly-elected candidate, a faction's votes go where those voters would choose if they had full information and coordination.

8.4.2 Numerical Example

Table 28 shows how the eight steps just listed produce the winners with the data used above, that is, with nine candidates for three vacant seats and 100 voters with the rankings shown in Table 24 submitting a valid ballot and voting sincerely.

The outcome in Table 28 contrasts sharply with what emerged with multi-winner plurality, limited voting, and cumulative voting.

With multi-winner plurality, the winners are likely to be (a) Abe, Ben, and Cal, (b) Dee, Eve, and Gil, or (c) Abe, Dee, and Eve. As indicated in Tables 25a and 25b, the associated values of the index of disproportionality are 0.56, 0.34, and 0.33, respectively.

With limited voting, the winners are likely to be (a) Dee, Eve, and Gil, or (b) Abe, Dee, and Eve. As indicated in Table 26, the associated values of the index of disproportionality are 0.34 and 0.33, respectively.

With cumulative voting, the winners are likely to be (a) Abe, Ben, and Cal, or (b) Dee, Eve, and Gil. As indicated in Table 27, the associated values of the index of disproportionality are 0.56 and 0.34, respectively.

In contrast, the winners with STV are likely to be Abe, Dee, and Gil. As Table 28 indicates, the associated value of the index of disproportionality is an unbeatable 0.02. This value is unbeatably low because there are three factions, each constitutes about ⅓ of the electorate, and the favorite candidate of each faction is elected. In turn, the favorite of each faction is elected because, with STV, votes automatically transfer to voters' next choices both when a candidate is elected with surplus votes and when a candidate is eliminated.

Table 28: Outcome with Single Transferable Vote

	Stage						
	1	2	3	4	5	6	7
Exhausted Ballots	0	0	0	32	32	32	67
Quota	$100 \cdot \frac{1}{3+1} = 25$	$100 \cdot \frac{1}{3+1} = 25$	$100 \cdot \frac{1}{3+1} = 25$	$(100-32) \cdot \frac{1}{3+1} = 17$	$(100-32) \cdot \frac{1}{3+1} = 17$	$(100-32) \cdot \frac{1}{3+1} = 17$	$(100-32) \cdot \frac{1}{3+1} = 17$
Votes for Abe	13	13	13	13	13	23	17
Votes for Ben	12	12	12	12	12	12	–
Votes for Cal	10	10	10	10	10	–	–
Votes for Dee	17	17	17	17	17	17	17
Votes for Eve	16	16	16	16	16	16	–
Votes for Fay	0	0	–	–	–	–	–
Votes for Gil	32	25	25	17	17	17	17
Votes for Hal	0	7	7	–	–	–	–
Votes for Ian	0	0	–	–	–	–	–
Votes not transferable	0	0	0	15	15	15	49
Total votes	100	100	100	100	100	100	100

Index of disproportionality for 3 factions when Abe, Dee, and Gil win is 0.0153.

Stage:

1: Because Gil has both more than a quota of votes and more votes than any other candidate, elect Gil; also, transfer Gil's surplus, (32 − 25 = 7 votes) to the next choice(s) on the 32 ballots where Gil was first choice, i.e. to Hal, and set Gil's tally at the quota.

2: Since no other candidate has more votes than the quota, start eliminating. Because both Fay and I an have no votes, eliminate both.

3: Now eliminate Hal, the next laggard. Because the 32 ballots that gave Hal 7 surplus votes now have no non-eliminated next choice, both the quota and Gil's tally (which is set at the quota) drop from 25 to 17 (and nontransferable votes rise from 0 to 15).

4: Because the quota dropped to 17 and Dee has at least that many votes, elect Dee. But, because Dee has exactly 17 votes, no additional transfer of surplus occurs here.

5: Eliminate Cal; transfer Cal's 10 votes to next choice(s) on the 10 ballots where Cal was first choice, i.e. to Abe.

6: Elect Abe and set Abe's tally at the quota. Since all three openings have now been filled, declare that Ben and Eve, along with Fay, Ian, Hal, and Cal, are defeated.

7: Crown Abe, Dee, and Gil.

8.4.3 Who Uses STV

Four countries use STV to elect part or all of their national legislatures. Australia was first. It has used STV to elect its national Senate since 1918. Every three years, each of Australia's six states fills six six-year Senate seats, and each of Australia's two territories fills two three-year seats (except that the number of open seats doubles if there is a "double dissolution").

The Republic of Malta was second. Although fully independent only since 1964, Malta has used STV to elect its national legislature (Kamra tad-Deputati), which is unicameral, since 1921. Each of 13 districts elects five representatives for a term of up to five years (except that, since 1981, the party whose candidates receive the most first-choices gets additional seats).

Third, the Republic of Ireland has used STV to elect its "lower" house (Dail Eireann) since gaining independence in 1922. There are 43 constituencies, each electing three, four, or five representatives for a term of up to five years. The ballot lists candidates in alphabetical order, regardless of party affiliation.

Fourth, India has used STV to elect its upper house (Rajya Sabha) since 1952. Of the 250 members, 238 are elected by the elected members of 30 state assemblies. Seats are allotted in proportion to the population of each state or union territory.

There are many other users: Australia's states and cities are users. STV is used to elect the "upper house" (Legislative Council) of (a) New South Wales (every four years, NSW fills 21 eight-year seats), (b) Victoria (every four years, each of eight electoral regions fills five four-year seats), (c) Australia(every four years, South Australia fills 11 four-year seats), and (d) Western Australia (every four years, each of six regions fills six four-year seats). In addition, STV is used to elect both (a) the "lower house" of Tasmania (every four years, each of five constituencies fills five four-year seats in the House of Assembly), and (b) the unicameral legislature of Australian Capital Territory (every four years, two constituencies fill five four-year seats in ACT's Legislative Assembly and one constituency fills seven). STV also is used in electing many local councils.

In Malta and Ireland, STV is used, not only when electing the national legislature, but also both in multi-winner local elections and when electing members of the European Parliament. (The European Union requires that MEPs be elected by a proportional system, and all other member states — including France and the UK, which traditionally use a single-winner system — use either a closed-list or an open-list system.)

Since 1973 Northern Ireland has used STV for all multi-winner elections except seats at Westminster.

Since 1941, Cambridge, MA, has used STV every two years to elect all nine members of its city council and all six members of its school committee.

New Zealand has used STV in local elections since 2004. Every three years, STV is used to fill seven three-year seats on each of 20 district health boards. In addition, STV is used to fill 13 to 15 three-year seats on seven city councils. For example, in Wellington (the capital), each of four wards fills three 3-year council seats every three years and one ward fills two (and a referendum in 2008 approved continuing to do so).

Since 2007, STV has been used to fill the three or four seats of a ward in each of Scotland's 32 local councils.

Since 2009, STV has been used to elect three of the nine members of the Minneapolis Park Board.

And STV is used to elect the student legislature at many universities in the U.S., Australia, and Britain (including UC Davis, University of California Berkeley, UCLA, Harvard, and MIT).

On the other hand, many other jurisdictions have rejected STV. From 1917 to 1962, Cincinnati, OH, Cleveland, OH, New York, and 18 other American cities started — and then stopped — using STV to elect their city councils. Advocates of STV attribute repeal to clawback by politicians and party bosses who lost power, hostility to election of blacks, portrayal of STV as communism, linkage with other components of a reform charter (such as employing a city manager), and disintegration of the progressive movement of the early 20th century.[11] In 2008, however, Cincinnati, OH voters again — by 5% — rejected STV despite a $100,000 campaign by FaiRVote (a Maryland-based non-profit that has promoted STV and IRV since 1992).

On the other hand, Irish voters recently voted to retain STV. In Jun-2013, the Convention on the Constitution of the Republic of Ireland considered replacing "our existing PR-STV system with MMP", and 79% voted No — but also voted to have at least five seats per STV constituency.

8.4.4 STV May Violate Monotonicity

The single transferable vote is a multi-winner version of instant runoff voting. If the total number of open seats in an STV election were reduced to one, then the rules of IRV would apply, and, when all but one of the open seats in an STV election have been filled, the rules of IRV do apply. So it should not be surprising that STV, like IRV, can violate monotonicity.

That is, it is possible that re-running an STV election will deprive a candidate of victory even though the only difference between the two elections is that, in the re-run, some voters raise the rank of the candidate who won initially. That result is perverse and unwelcome. To see how and why it can occur, we will compare two cases — one before and the other after two voters raise the rank of a candidate while retaining the order in which they rank all other candidates.

Suppose that there are two open seats, five candidates (namely, Abe, Ben, Cal, Dee, and Eve), and 30 ballots with the rankings shown in Table 29a.

---

[11]See (1) Kathleen L. Barber, Proportional Representation and Election Reform in Ohio, Ohio State University Press, 1995, and (2) Douglas J. Amy, Real Choices / New Voices, Columbia University Press, 2nd ed., 2002.

Table 29a: Rankings Before Two Voters Raise Ben's Rank

Rankings of Candidates	Number of Ballots with That Ranking:
Abe >Ben >Cal >Dee >Eve	16
Abe >Cal >Ben >Dee >Eve	1
Cal >Ben >Dee >Eve	6
Dee >Cal >Ben >Eve	5
Eve >Dee >Cal >Ben	2
Total	30

Given those 30 ballots, STV elects Abe at Stage 1 and Ben at Stage 4. Table 29b shows the calculations.

To calculate the Index of Disproportionality for five factions when Abe and Ben win, we do the following calculations where S is the proportion of seats received and V is the proportion of votes received:

$$I_D = \sqrt{\frac{1}{2} \cdot \sum_{factions} (S - V)^2}$$

$$= \sqrt{\frac{1}{2} \cdot \left(\left(\frac{1}{2} - \frac{17}{30}\right)^2 + \left(\frac{0}{2} - \frac{6}{30}\right)^2 + \left(\frac{0}{2} - \frac{5}{30}\right)^2 + \left(\frac{0}{2} - \frac{2}{30}\right)^2 + \left(\frac{1}{2} - \frac{0}{30}\right)^2 \right)}$$

$$= \sqrt{\frac{1}{2} \cdot \left((0.5 - 0.566667)^2 + (0 - 0.2)^2 + (0 - 0.166667)^2 + (0 - 0.06667)^2 + (0.5 - 0)^2 \right)}$$

$$= \sqrt{\frac{1}{2} \cdot \left(-0.06667^2 + -0.2^2 + -0.166667^2 + -0.06667^2 + 0.5^2 \right)}$$

$$= \sqrt{\frac{1}{2} \cdot (0.00444 + 0.04 + 0.027778 + 0.00444 + 0.25)}$$

$$= \sqrt{.5 \cdot 0.32667}$$

$$= 0.4041$$

Now suppose that it is still true that those five candidates are eligible for two open seats and 30 voters submit a valid ballot — but that the 30 ballots now have the rankings shown in Table 30a.

Note that 28 of the 30 voters have the same rankings in both cases, while two voters rank Ben higher in the second case than the first but make no change in the order of

Table 29b: Outcome Before Two Voters Raise Ben's Rank

	Stage				
	1	2	3	4	5
Exhausted Ballots	0	0	0	0	0
Quota	$30 \cdot \frac{1}{2+1} = 10$	$30 \cdot \frac{1}{2+1} = 10$	$30 \cdot \frac{1}{2+1} = 10$	$30 \cdot \frac{1}{2+1} = 10$	$30 \cdot \frac{1}{2+1} = 10$
Votes for Abe	17	10.0	10.0	10.0	10.0
Votes for Ben	0	6.6	6.6	13.0	10.0
Votes for Cal	6	6.4	6.4	–	–
Votes for Dee	5	5	7	7	–
Votes for Eve	2	2	–	–	–
Votes not transferable	0	0	0	0	10.0
Total votes	30	30	30	30	30

Stage:

1: Because Abe has both more than a quota of votes and more votes than any other candidate, elect Abe; also, transfer Abe's surplus, i.e. $17 - 10.0 = 7.0$ votes, to the next choice(s) on the 17 ballots where Abe was first choice, i.e. to Ben and Cal, and set Abe's tally at the quota, that is, at 10.0. Of Abe's 7-vote surplus, Ben receives $7.0 \cdot \frac{16}{17} = 6.6$ votes and Cal receives $7.0 \cdot \frac{1}{17} = 0.4$.

2: Because no other candidate has more than a quota of votes and Eve has the fewest votes, eliminate Eve. Then transfer Eve's 2 votes to the next not-yet-eliminated choice(s) on the 2 ballots where Eve was top choice, i.e. to Dee. That raises Dee's tally from 5 votes to 7.

3: Because no other candidate has at least a quota of votes and Cal has the fewest votes, eliminate Cal. Then transfer Cal's 6.4 votes to the next not-yet-eliminated choice(s) on the 7 ballots where Cal was top choice, i.e. to Ben. That raises Ben's tally from 6.6 to 13.0.

4: Because Ben has both at least a quota of votes and more votes than any other candidate who has not yet been elected or eliminated, elect Ben and set Ben's tally at the quota, that is, at 10.0.

5: Crown Abe and Ben.

Table 30a: Rankings After Two Voters Raise Ben's Rank

Rankings of Candidates	Number of Voters with that Ranking:	
Abe >Ben >Cal >Dee >Eve	16	(as before)
Abe >Cal >Ben >Dee >Eve	1	(as before)
Cal >Ben >Dee >Eve	6	(as before)
Dee >Cal >Ben >Eve	5	(as before)
Ben >Eve >Dee >Cal	2	(Ben elevated)
	Total 30	

candidates other than Ben. Nevertheless, the winners are now Abe and Cal, not Abe and Ben. Table 30b shows the calculations.

To calculate the Index of Disproportionality for four factions when Abe and Cal win, we do the following calculations where S is the proportion of seats received and V is the proportion of votes received:

$$I_D = \sqrt{\frac{1}{2} \cdot \sum_{factions} (S - V)^2}$$

$$= \sqrt{\frac{1}{2} \cdot \left(\left(\frac{1}{2} - \frac{17}{30}\right)^2 + \left(\frac{1}{2} - \frac{6}{30}\right)^2 + \left(\frac{0}{2} - \frac{5}{30}\right)^2 + \left(\frac{0}{2} - \frac{2}{30}\right)^2 \right)}$$

$$= \sqrt{\frac{1}{2} \cdot \left((0.5 - 0.566667)^2 + (0.5 - 0.2)^2 + (0 - 0.166667)^2 + (0 - 0.06667)^2 \right)}$$

$$= \sqrt{\frac{1}{2} \cdot (-0.06667^2 + 0.3^2 + -0.166667^2 + -0.06667^2)}$$

$$= \sqrt{\frac{1}{2} \cdot (0.00444 + 0.09 + 0.027778 + 0.00444)}$$

$$= \sqrt{0.5 \cdot 0.06333}$$

$$= 0.2517$$

In other words, raising Ben's rank Ben deprived Ben of victory, and that violates monotonicity. An election system that is monotonic will never deprive a candidate of victory when some voters assign a higher rank to that candidate while making no change in the order of other candidates.

Table 30b: Outcome After Two Voters Raise Ben's Rank

	Stage				
	1	2	3	4	5
Exhausted Ballots	0	0	0	0	0
Quota	$30 \cdot \frac{1}{2+1} = 10$	$30 \cdot \frac{1}{2+1} = 10$	$30 \cdot \frac{1}{2+1} = 10$	$30 \cdot \frac{1}{2+1} = 10$	$30 \cdot \frac{1}{2+1} = 10$
Votes for Abe	17	10.0	10.0	10.0	10.0
Votes for Ben	2	8.6	8.6	8.6	–
Votes for Cal	6	6.4	6.4	11.4	10.0
Votes for Dee	5	5	5	–	–
Votes for Eve	0	0	–	–	–
Votes not transferable	0	0	0	0	10.0
Total votes	30	30	30	30	30

Stage:

1: Because Abe has both more than a quota of votes and more votes than any other candidate, elect Abe; also, transfer Abe's surplus, i.e. $17 - 10.0 = 7.0$ votes, to the next choice(s) on the 17 ballots where Abe was first choice, i.e. to Ben and Cal, and set Abe's tally at the quota, that is, at 10.0. Of Abe's 7-vote surplus, Ben receives $7.0 \cdot \frac{16}{17} = 6.6$ votes and Cal receives $7.0 \cdot \frac{1}{17} = 0.4$.

2: Because no other candidate has more than a quota of votes and Eve has the fewest votes (namely, 0) eliminate Eve.

3: Because no other candidate has at least a quota of votes and Dee has the fewest votes, eliminate Dee. Then transfer Dee's 5 votes to the next not-yet-eliminated choice(s) on the 5 ballots where Dee was top choice, i.e. to Cal. That raises Cal's tally from 6.4 to 11.4.

4: Because Cal has both at least a quota of votes and more votes than any other candidate who has not yet been elected or eliminated, elect Cal and set Cal's tally at the quota, that is, at 10.0.

5: Crown Abe and Cal.

8.4.5 STV vs IRV

Although STV is a multi-winner version of IRV,the two systems are not equivalent. The outcome is likely to be very different if a number of single-member districts using IRV are merged into a smaller number of constituencies that elect the same total number of representatives but do so with STV. Similarly, the outcome is likely to be very different if a number of multi-member constituencies using STV are divided into a larger number of single-member districts that elect the same total number of representatives with IRV.

The outcome is likely to change in this situations because STV is designed to produce proportionality among factions within a district, while IRV — or any other single-winner system — is inherently disproportional within a district and, if accompanied by gerrymandering, may be deliberately disproportional among a group of districts.

Results for the Australian Greens provide an illustration. In August 2010, there were eight elections to Australia's national Senate, each having multiple winners chosen by STV, and 150 elections to the national House of Representatives, each having one winner chosen by IRV. Overall, the electorate were the same.

In the House contests, a ballot was valid only if the voter ranked all of the district's candidates, and Green candidates were first choice on 11.4% of the ballots. In the Senate contests, where a voter could either rank all candidates or choose the ranking recommended by a political party, over 95% of voters in fact chose a party's ranking, and 13.1% of those voters chose the Greens' list. So approximately 12% of the electorate favored the Greens.

What were the outcomes? Green candidates won one seat in each of the six states (and won no seats in the two territories), a total of six (15.0%) of 40 open Senate seats. In the House elections, however, Greens won only one (0.7%) of the 150 open seats. In the House, therefore, the Greens were under-represented, and the reason is that each district chose one representative in a single-winner election , instead of choosing multiple representatives by a method intended to produce proportional representation.

On such evidence, some legal scholars have concluded that STV is the best way to implement the U.S. Voting Rights Act.[12]

8.5 Multiple Transferable Vote (MTV)

8.5.1 How the System Selects the Winners

An election is held to fill two or more positions in a legislative chamber. An official ballot (a) states how many positions are open, (b) lists individuals eligible to win a position, (c) perhaps invites write-ins, and (d) invites each voter to rank the candidates in order of preference, perhaps by assigning the number 1 to the candidate they most prefer, 2 to their second choice, 3 to their third choice, etc.

---

[12]See, for example, S. Mulroy, Voting Rights Act Remedies, 77 N.C.L.Rev. 1867 (1999).

The official ballot also says that (e) each valid ballot will cast as many votes as there are openings, (f) all of a voter's votes initially will go to that voter's first choice, and (g) any of those votes not used to elect that first choice will automatically transfer to that voter's second choice, and then to that voter's third choice, and so on until all used up.

The procedure used to determine the outcome with multiple transferable vote is the same as with single transferable vote (see the eight steps listed above), and results with MTV are the same as results with STV.

8.5.2 Numerical Example

Table 31 shows how MTV determines the winners in the circumstances repeatedly discussed above, that is, with nine candidates for three vacant seats and 100 voters with the rankings shown in Table 24 submitting a valid ballot and voting sincerely.

Note that results with MTV are the same as with STV. Specifically, again Abe, Dee, and Gil win. In addition, there is no change in the number of stages needed to determine which candidates win or in the stage at which each candidate is elected or eliminated.

Switching from STV to MTV did change the numerical value of several variables. In particular, change occurred in (a) the quota (that is, the number of votes needed to be elected), (b) the candidates' tallies (that is, the number of votes that, after transfers of votes that occurred at previous steps, each candidate currently has), and (c) the number of untransferable votes (that is, votes that, because some ballots have incomplete rankings, cannot be transferred from elected or eliminated candidates to active candidates). However, switching to MTV changed the numerical values of these three variables exactly in proportion to the change in the number of votes per ballot; specifically, the quota, tallies, and untransferable votes were, at every stage, three times their values with STV.

8.5.3 MTV vs. STV

If MTV has the same procedure and the same outcome as STV, then why distinguish the two? Here are three reasons.

First, MTV avoids an objection to STV. Every two years, multi-winner plurality is used to fill either two or three seats on the city council of Davis, California, and an attempt to change to STV failed after opponents of STV (including an influential but numerically-challenged local columnist) asserted that using STV would deprive voters of their second and third votes. Advocates of STV implicitly conceded that point by referring to a single vote and then — fruitlessly — trying to explain how a single vote could support more than one candidate. Because MTV, unlike STV, would allow voters to continue to cast as many votes as there are open seats, MTV is more likely than STV to gain public approval.

Second, MTV can be viewed as an improved version of cumulative voting. Cumulative voting does not enable a minority or other faction to obtain proportional representation unless the faction knows how many votes it will cast and optimally allocates those votes

Table 31: Outcome with Multiple Transferable Vote

	Stage						
	1	2	3	4	5	6	7
Exhausted Ballots	0	0	0	32	32	32	67
Quota	$3 \cdot 100 \cdot \frac{1}{3+1} = 75.0$	$3 \cdot 100 \cdot \frac{1}{3+1} = 75.0$	$3 \cdot 100 \cdot \frac{1}{3+1} = 75.0$	$3 \cdot (100-32) \cdot \frac{1}{3+1} = 51.0$	$3 \cdot (100-32) \cdot \frac{1}{3+1} = 51.0$	$3 \cdot (100-32) \cdot \frac{1}{3+1} = 51.0$	$3 \cdot (100-32) \cdot \frac{1}{3+1} = 51.0$
Votes for Abe	39	39	39	39	39	69	51.0
Votes for Ben	36	36	36	36	36	36	–
Votes for Cal	30	30	30	30	30	–	–
Votes for Dee	51	51	51	51	51	51	51
Votes for Eve	48	48	48	48	48	48	–
Votes for Fay	0	0	–	–	–	–	–
Votes for Gil	96	75	75	51	51	51	51
Votes for Hal	0	21	21	–	–	–	–
Votes for Ian	0	0	–	–	–	–	–
Votes not transferable	0	0	0	45	45	45	147
Total votes	300	300	300	300	300	300	300

Index of disproportionality for 3 factions when Abe, Dee, and Gil win is 0.0153.

Stage:

1: Because Gil has both more than a quota of votes and more votes than any other candidate, elect Gil; also, transfer Gil's surplus, i.e. $96 - 75.0 = 21.0$ votes, to the next choice(s) on the 32 ballots where Gil was first choice, i.e. to Hal, and set Gil's tally at the quota.

2: Since no other candidate has at least a quota of votes, start eliminating. Because both Fay and Ian have no votes, eliminate both.

3: Now eliminate Hal, the next laggard. Because the 32 ballots that gave Hal 21 surplus votes now have no non-eliminated next choice, both the quota and Gil's tally (which is set at the quota) drop from 75.0 to 51.0 (and nontransferable votes rise from 0 to 45.0).

4: Because the quota dropped to 51.0 and Dee has at least that many votes, elect Dee. But, because Dee has exactly 51 votes, no additional transfer of surplus occurs here.

5: Eliminate Cal; transfer Cal's 30 votes to next choice(s) on the 10 ballots where Cal was first choice, i.e. to Abe.

6: Elect Abe and set Abe's tally at the quota. Since all three openings have now been filled, declare that Ben and Eve, along with Fay, Ian, Hal, and Cal, are defeated.

7: Crown Abe, Dee, and Gil.

among the candidates. With MTV, in contrast, votes are automatically distributed as voters would choose if they knew how others were voting. As a result, people who like cumulative voting and see no analogy between it and STV may find MTV both analogous and appealing.

Third, because MTV is, in a sense, an improved version of cumulative voting, MTV can reasonably take the place of cumulative voting as a remedy in voting-rights cases. In other words, when multi-winner plurality is held to violate the Federal or California Voting Rights Act, the remedy of choice might well be MTV, not cumulative voting — and not limited voting or single-representative districts.

8.5.4 Who Uses MTV

No users — at least not yet.

8.6 Constrained Single or Multiple Transferable Vote

8.6.1 How the System Selects the Winners

An election is held to fill two or more positions in a legislative chamber, and there is at least one restriction on which candidates may win. For example, the rules may require that at least one winner be male.

An official ballot states how many positions are open, lists individuals eligible to win a position, invites each voter to rank the candidates in order of preference, and perhaps mentions the restrictions that have been placed on the outcome.

The restrictions are implemented by forbidding any selection or elimination of a candidate to occur that would cause a restriction to be violated. With that qualification, voters' rankings are converted to seats won in a way that, as with unconstrained STV or MTV, is intended to make the proportion of seats won by each faction's favorites as close as possible to the proportion of votes cast by that faction.

8.6.2 Numerical Example

In the case repeatedly discussed above, nine candidates vie for three vacant seats and 100 voters with the rankings shown in Table 24 vote sincerely. Suppose that the rules state that at least one winner must be a woman. Suppose also that, of the nine candidates, four are women, namely, Bev, Cas, Eve, and Fay. Table 32 shows how, with the constraint, MTV determines the outcome.

In Table 32, ballot-processing proceeds as in Table 31 until Stage 5. At that point, three female candidates, namely, Bev, Cas, and Eve, along with Abe (a man) are the only continuing candidates. Because at least one winner must be a woman, Abe is now eliminated. Transfer of Abe's votes then puts Bev over the top.

Table 32: Outcome with Multiple Transferable Vote When At Least One of Bev, Cas, Eve and Fay Must Win

	Stage						
	1	2	3	4	5	6	7
Exhausted Ballots	0	0	0	32	32	32	67
Quota	$3 \cdot 100 \cdot \frac{1}{3+1} = 75.0$	$3 \cdot 100 \cdot \frac{1}{3+1} = 75.0$	$3 \cdot 100 \cdot \frac{1}{3+1} = 75.0$	$3 \cdot (100 - 32) \cdot \frac{1}{3+1} = 51.0$	$3 \cdot (100 - 32) \cdot \frac{1}{3+1} = 51.0$	$3 \cdot (100 - 32) \cdot \frac{1}{3+1} = 51.0$	$3 \cdot (100 - 32) \cdot \frac{1}{3+1} = 51.0$
Votes for Abe	39	39	39	39	39	–	–
Votes for Bev	36	36	36	36	36	75	51
Votes for Cas	30	30	30	30	30	30	–
Votes for Dan	51	51	51	51	51	51	51
Votes for Eve	48	48	48	48	48	48	–
Votes for Fay	0	0	–	–	–	–	–
Votes for Gil	96	75	75	51	51	51	51
Votes for Hal	0	21	21	–	–	–	–
Votes for Ian	0	0	–	–	–	–	–
Votes not transferable	0	0	0	45	45	45	147
Total votes	300	300	300	300	300	300	300

Index of disproportionality for 3 factions when Abe, Dan, and Gil win is 0.0153.

Stage:
1: Because Gil has both more than a quota of votes and more votes than any other candidate, elect Gil; also, transfer Gil's surplus, i.e. $96 - 75.0 = 21.0$ votes, to the next choice(s) on the 32 ballots where Gil was first choice, i.e. to Hal, and set Gil's tally at the quota.
2: Since no other candidate has at least a quota of votes, start eliminating. Because both Fay and Ian have no votes, eliminate both.
3: Now eliminate Hal, the next laggard. Because the 32 ballots that gave Hal 21 surplus votes now have no non-eliminated next choice, both the quota and Gil's tally (which is set at the quota) drop from 75.0 to 51.0 (and nontransferable votes rise from 0 to 45.0).
4: Because the quota dropped to 51.0 and Dan has at least that many votes, elect Dan. But, because Dan has exactly 51 votes, no additional transfer of surplus occurs here.
5: Because only one seat remains unfilled, at least one of Bev, Cas, Eve, and Fay must win, Fay has been eliminated, and none of Bev, Cas, and Eve has at least a quota of votes, eliminate all candidates except Bev, Cas, and Eve, that is eliminate Abe. Also, transfer Abe's 39 votes to the next choice(s) on the 13 ballots where Abe was first choice, i.e. to Bev.
6: Because Bev now has at least a quota of votes, elect Bev and set Bev's tally at the current quota.
7: Crown Bev, Dan, and Gil.

Ordinarily, the index of disproportionality will rise when a constraint alters the outcome, Here, however, Dan and Eve are favored by the same faction, and the index does not take account of how many voters prefer Dan to Eve and vice versa. As a result, the index remains 0.02.

8.6.3 Who Uses STV or MTV with constraints

There may be restrictions on who is elected. For example, seats are reserved for Christians in Palestine, for Hungarians and Italians in Slovenia, and for eight different minorities in Croatia. While none of these elections uses a transferable vote, there has been at least one STV election with constraints on the outcome.

In June 2010, Britain's parliament used STV with two constraints to elect three deputy speakers. One constraint was that two of the three winners must be Labour MPs. The other constraint was that at least one of the three winners must be a woman.

Both constraints affected the outcome. One at a time, three trailing candidates, including the lone Conservative female (McIntosh), were eliminated and their votes transferred to continuing candidates. Then a Conservative male (Evans) was elected and his surplus transferred to continuing candidates. Then, in order to save a seat for a woman and a seat for a Labour MP, two Conservative males were excluded and their votes transferred. Then a Labour male was eliminated and his votes transferred. Then a Labour male (Hoyle) was elected and his surplus transferred. That left two candidates. One of the two (Primarolo) was elected both because she was a Labour female and because she had the larger tally.

8.7 Closed-List Voting (also known as "Closed-List Representation" and "Closed Party-List Proportional Representation")

8.7.1 How the System Selects the Winners

An election is held to fill two or more positions in a legislative chamber, and political parties or coalitions prepare lists of candidates. An official ballot identifies either the lists or the parties that prepared them and tells each voter to choose one. For each valid ballot on which one is chosen, that list receives one "vote".

A list wins seats only if its proportion of the total vote exceeds a predetermined hurdle, called the "threshold". In practice, the threshold ranges from 0 in Scotland, South Africa, and Wales to 10% in Turkey, the most frequent choice elsewhere (for example, in Germany, New Zealand, Russia, and Thailand) being 5%. A particular individual is elected only if everyone higher on the same list also is elected.

In some countries — for example, Belgium, Israel, and Uruguay — parties are allowed to form alliances. With this arrangement, called "apparentement electoral", the ballot still lists the allied parties separately. But, hoping to elect an extra — or at least one — candidate, the parties formally agree to pool their spare votes.

8.7.2   D'Hondt and Sainte-Laguë rules

In addition to having different thresholds, different countries have different rules for translating votes into seats. Two rules are in common use. When there are, say, q lists that exceed the threshold and n open seats, both rules utilize $q \cdot n$ numbers — but obtain them differently.

Belgian mathematician Victor D'Hondt (pronounced "Dahnt") proposed one of the two rules.[13] With the D'Hondt rule, officials obtain the $q \cdot n$ numbers by dividing the number of votes received by each of the q qualifying lists first by 1, then by 2, then by 3, then by 4, and so on up to the number of seats that are open, that is, n.

French mathematician André Sainte-Laguë (pronounced "Saint Lagoo") proposed the other rule.[14] With the Sainte-Laguë rule, officials obtain the $q \cdot n$ numbers by dividing the number of votes received by each of the q qualifying lists first by 1, then by 3, then by 5, then by 7, and so on up to $2 \cdot (n - 1) + 1$.

There is also a modified Sainte-Laguë rule. Norway uses it to implement a closed-list system, and Sweden uses it to implement an open-list system. With this version, which they call "the adjusted odd-number method", the first divisor is 1.4 instead of 1.0, while the next divisors are the standard 3, 5, 7, etc.

With any of the three rules for converting votes to seats, officials identify the n largest of the $q \cdot n$ quotients. If a particular list has, say, k of those n largest quotients, then officials award k seats to that list.

8.7.3   Numerical Example

Eight seats are open; 250,000 votes are cast; the threshold is 4%, that is, 10,000 votes; and four lists receive at least that 4% while two lists do not. Specifically, List Ape receives 110,000 votes; List Bear receives 80,000; List Cat receives 30,000; List Dog receives 20,000; List Elk receives 6,000; and List Fox receives 4,000.

Because eight seats are open and four lists passed the threshold, officials determine 32 quotients, then identify the eight largest of those 32 quotients, and then assign the eight open seats to the individual lists. Table 33a shows the outcome if the quotients are obtained using the D'Hondt divisors.

To calculate Gallagher's index of disproportionality, we perform the following steps

---

[13]V. D'Hondt, La repr'sentation proportionnelle des partis par un électeur, Ghent, 1878.

[14]A. Sainte-Laguë, "La Representation Proportionelle et la Methode des Moindres Carres," Comptes Rendus Hebdomaires des Seances de l'Academie des Sciences, 151: 377–78, 1910.

Table 33a: Outcome with 4% Threshold and D'Hondt Rule

	Ape	Bear	Cat	Dog	Elk	Fox	Total
Votes Received	110,000	80,000	30,000	20,000	6,000	4,000	250,000
Percentage of 250,000 Votes	44.0%	32.0%	12.0%	8.0%	2.4%	1.6%	100.0%
D'Hondt Divisor		Votes Received ÷D'Hondt Divisor					
1	110,000.0	80,000.0	30,000.0	20,000.0			
2	55,000.0	40,000.0	15,000.0	10,000.0			
3	36,666.7	26,666.7	10,000.0	6,666.7			
4	27,500.0	20,000.0	7,500.0	5,000.0			
5	22,000.0	16,000.0	6,000.0	4,000.0			
6	18,333.3	13,333.3	5,000.0	3,333.3			
7	15,714.3	11,428.6	4,285.7	2,857.1			
8	13,750.0	10,000.0	3,750.0	2,500.0			
Number of Seats Awarded	4	3	1	0	0	0	8
Percentage of 8 Seats	50.0%	37.5%	12.5%	0.0%	0.0%	0.0%	100.0%

where S is the proportion of seats won and V is the proportion of votes received:

$$I_D = \sqrt{\frac{1}{2} \sum_{parties} (S - V)^2}$$

$$\sum_{parties} (S - V)^2 = \left[\left(\frac{4}{8} - \frac{100}{250}\right)^2 + \left(\frac{3}{8} - \frac{80}{250}\right)^2 + \left(\frac{1}{8} - \frac{30}{250}\right)^2 + \left(\frac{0}{8} - \frac{20}{250}\right)^2 + \right.$$

$$\left. \left(\frac{0}{8} - \frac{6}{250}\right)^2 + \left(\frac{0}{8} - \frac{4}{250}\right)^2 \right]$$

$$\sum_{parties} (S - V)^2 = \left[(0.5 - 0.44)^2 + (0.375 - 0.32)^2 + (0.125 - 0.12)^2 + (0.0 - 0.08)^2 + \right.$$

$$\left. (0.0 - 0.024)^2 + (0.0 - 0.016)^2 \right]$$

$$\sum_{parties} (S - V)^2 = \left[0.06^2 + 0.55^2 + 0.005^2 + -0.08^2 + -0.024^2 + -0.016^2 \right]$$

$$\sum_{parties} (S - V)^2 = \left[0.0036 + 0.003025 + 0.000025 + 0.0064 + 0.000576 + 0.000256 \right]$$

$$\sum_{parties} (S - V)^2 = 0.013882$$

$$I_D = \sqrt{0.5 \cdot 0.013882}$$
$$I_D = \sqrt{0.006941}$$
$$I_D = 0.0833$$

Table 33a indicates that, with the D'Hondt rule , four of the eight largest quotients (namely, 110,000, 55,000, 36,667, and 27,500) belong to List Ape, while three (namely, 80,000, 40,000, and 26,667) belong to List Bear, and one (namely, 30,000) belongs to List Cat. Hence, none belongs to List Dog. Accordingly, with the D'Hondt rule, List Ape's top four are elected, along with List Bear's top three and the top one on List Cat's list.

Table 33b shows the outcome if, instead, officials use the Sainte-Laguë divisors. With the Sainte-Laguë rule , only three of the eight largest quotients (namely, 110,000, 36,667, and 22,000) belong to List Ape. The next three (namely, 80,000, 26,667, and 16,000) belong to List Bear, while one (namely, 30,000) belongs to List Cat and one (namely, 20,000) belongs to List Dog. Accordingly, with the Sainte-Laguë rule , List Ape's top three are elected, along with List Bear's top three, the top one of List Cat, and the top one of List Dog.

Table 33b: Outcome with 4% Threshold and Sainte-Laguë Rule

	Ape	Bear	Cat	Dog	Elk	Fox	Total
Votes Received	110,000	80,000	30,000	20,000	6,000	4,000	250,000
Percentage of 250,000 Votes	44.0%	32.0%	12.0%	8.0%	2.4%	1.6%	100.0%
Sainte-Laguë Divisor	Votes Received ÷ Sainte-Laguë Divisor						
1	110,000.0	80,000.0	30,000.0	20,000.0			
3	36,666.7	26,666.7	10,000.0	6,666.7			
5	22,000.0	16,000.0	6,000.0	4,000.0			
7	15,714.3	11,428.6	4,285.7	2,857.1			
9	12,222.2	8,888.9	3,333.3	2,222.2			
11	10,000.0	7,272.7	2,727.3	1,818.2			
13	8,461.5	6,153.8	2,307.7	1,538.5			
15	7,333.3	5,333.3	2,000.0	1,333.3			
Number of Seats Awarded	3	3	1	1	0	0	8
Percentage of 8 Seats	37.5%	37.5%	12.5%	12.5%	0.0%	0.0%	100.0%

Gallagher's index of disproportionality = 0.0712

As Tables 33a and 33b indicate, the Sainte-Laguë rule is more favorable than the D'Hondt rule to small parties or coalitions and therefore tends to produce greater proportionality. Of the eight open seats, Lists Ape, Bear, Cat, and Dog win 50%, 37.5%, 12.5%, and 0 with the D'Hondt rule and 37.5%, 37.5%, 12.5%, and 12.5% with the Sainte-Laguë rule. As a result, Gallagher's index of disproportionality decreases from 0.08 with the D'Hondt rule to 0.07 with the Sainte-Laguë rule.

Table 33c shows what outcome emerges if, instead, officials use the modified Sainte-Laguë divisors. Note that, with the modified Sainte-Laguë divisors as with the D'Hondt divisors, List Dog receives no seat. As this illustrates, it is less likely with the modified than with the original Sainte-Laguë rule that the first quotient of a minor party will be large enough to produce a seat. In fact, that was the reason for the modification.

Table 33c: Outcome with 4% Threshold and Modified Sainte-Laguë Rule

	Ape	Bear	Cat	Dog	Elk	Fox	Total
Votes Received	110,000	80,000	30,000	20,000	6,000	4,000	250,000
Percentage of 250,000 Votes	44.0%	32.0%	12.0%	8.0%	2.4%	1.6%	100.0%
Modified Sainte-Laguë Divisor	Votes Received ÷Modified Sainte-Laguë Divisor						
1.4	78571.4	57142.9	21428.6	14285.7			
3	36666.7	26666.7	10000.0	6666.7			
5	22000.0	16000.0	6000.0	4000.0			
7	15714.3	11428.6	4285.7	2857.1			
9	12222.2	8888.9	3333.3	2222.2			
11	10000.0	7272.7	2727.3	1818.2			
13	8461.5	6153.8	2307.7	1538.5			
15	7333.3	5333.3	2000.0	1333.3			
Number of Seats Awarded	4	3	1	0	0	0	8
Percentage of 8 Seats	50.0%	37.5%	12.5%	0.0%	0.0%	0.0%	100.0%

Gallagher's index of disproportionality = 0.0833

8.7.4 Who Uses Closed Lists

Closed lists are used in electing part or all of many national legislatures. Bosnia, Germany, New Zealand, and Poland implement a closed-list system with the Sainte-Laguë rule.

On the other hand, the D'Hondt rule is used in Albania, Argentina, Austria, Belgium, Bulgaria, Colombia, Croatia, Czech Republic, East Timor, Ecuador, Estonia, Iceland, Israel, Macedonia, Moldova, Montenegro, Northern Ireland, Paraguay, Peru, Portugal, Romania, Scotland, Serbia, Slovenia, South Africa, Spain, Turkey, and Uruguay.

Do not infer that the proportionality of a closed-list system depends only on whether the D'Hondt or Sainte-Laguë rule is used. With either rule, proportionality tends to increase if (a) the threshold is lowered, or (b) the number of open seats is increased, or (c) small parties can form alliances, or (d) there is just one election district (as is the case when Israel, Moldova, Namibia, the Netherlands, and Slovakia elect their national legislatures).

Incidentally, the U.S. could use the D'Hondt or Sainte-Laguë rule to allocate seats in the House of Representatives—but does not. Instead, each state has at least one seat. To acknowledge differences in population, we have, since 1941, used the "method of equal proportions", proposed by American mathematicians Joseph Hill and Edward Huntington.[15]

8.7.5 Who Prepares Party Lists

How do parties or coalitions prepare their lists of candidates? In Belgium and Sweden, the Pirate Party conducts a multi-winner primary election. That, however, is unusual.

Usually a party's elected leaders and important supporters prepare their party's lists on their own. For electoral success, however, the party elite often needs both to offer geographical and ethnic balance and to recognize the seniority and popularity of various prominent individuals. In addition, there may be legal constraints on a list of candidates; for example, Belgium requires one man and one woman in the first two slots on a list, and Bolivia requires that the genders alternate throughout a list.

8.8 Open-List Voting (also known as "Open-List Proportional Representation" and "Open-List Proportional Representation")

8.8.1 How the System Selects the Winners

An election is held to fill two or more positions in a legislative chamber, and political parties or coalitions prepare lists of individual candidates. An official ballot identifies those parties or lists and tells each voter to indicate a preference either (a) for a party

---

[15]Huntington, E.V., "The Mathematical Theory of the Apportionment of Representatives", Proceedings of the National Academy of Sciences, U.S. A., 7:123'127, 1921.

or list, or (b) in an indented paragraph beneath the name of a party or list, for up to a specified number of individuals on the party's list (and therefore, implicitly, for that party). Alternatively, a voter is offered a separate ballot-sheet for each list and is told (a) to indicate a preference for individuals listed on one of those sheets, and (b) to put that sheet a ballot-box and discard the other sheets.

Rules that vary from country to country determine (a) the number of individuals for whom a voter may indicate a preference, and (b) how many preference-votes an individual must receive in order to be elected ahead of candidates ranked higher on a party's list.

As with a closed-list election, votes for a party usually are converted to seats in the legislature by either the D'Hondt rule or the Sainte-Laguë rule. However, the proportion of the total vote that a party must receive in order to receive a seat varies from country to country. For example, the Netherlands has a single, nationwide election district with a threshold of 0.67%, while Sweden has a threshold of 12% in each of 29 electoral districts (and a threshold of 4% for 39 "adjustment" seats awarded according to parties' nationwide vote).

8.8.2 Numerical Example

Suppose that (a) a political party receives enough votes to win five seats in a legislature, (b) an individual on the party's list who receives at least 250 preference-votes is to be elected ahead of individuals who, although higher on the list, receive fewer preference-votes, and (c) the third column in Table 34 shows how many preference-votes in fact were received by individuals on the party's list. Then the winners will be as show in the fifth column of the table.

Table 34: Who Moves Up an Open List

	Position on Party's List	Number of Preference Votes Received	Revised Rank	Elected?	Because
Abe	1	3500	1	Yes	With most preference-votes, remains #1.
Ben	2	50	4	Yes	Only 3 others have at least 250 preference-votes.
Cal	3	150	5	Yes	Only 3 others have at least 250 preference-votes.
Dee	4	250	3	Yes	Received enough preference-votes to move up.
Eve	5	100	6	No	Pushed out of top 5.
Fay	6	100	7	No	Never among top 5.
Gil	7	450	2	Yes	Received enough preference-votes to move up.
Hal	8	50	8	No	Never among top 5.

Note that Eve is not elected despite being fifth on the party's list and having more preference votes than Ben, who is elected.

8.8.3   Who uses Open Lists

Though less common than closed lists, open lists are not rare. They are used in electing the national legislatures of Brazil, Chile, Cyprus, Denmark, Finland, Iceland, Indonesia, Iraq, Japan, Kosovo, Latvia, Luxembourg, the Netherlands, Norway, Slovakia, Sri Lanka, Sweden, and Switzerland — but in some cases merely as part of a mixed-member election system.

How the individual winners are chosen varies from country to country. Here are some of the variations:

In the Netherlands, an individual receiving at least 25% of the number of votes that a party needs to win one seat precedes individuals who were higher on the party's list but receive fewer preference-votes.

In elections to Sweden's Riksdag, individuals receiving at least 8% of a party's votes in an election district move to the top of the party's list for that constituency, arranged there in order of the number of preference-votes that each received.

In Slovakia, a voter may select up to four individuals on a party's list, and individuals selected by more than 3% of a party's voters are — in order of votes received — elected ahead of others on the party's list.

In Switzerland and Luxembourg, a voter can cast as many votes are there are open seats, can cast from one to all of those votes for a single individual (as with cumulative voting), and can vote for individuals on more than one list.

In elections for Brazil's "lower" house (Chamber of Deputies) and for Finland's unicameral Eduskunta, each voter casts one vote. In each of Brazil's 26 states, the vote may be cast either for a list or for a listed individual but, in Finland, which has 15 election districts , only for a listed individual. To determine how many seats a particular list wins in a particular district, the D'Hondt rule is applied in Finland to the total number of votes received by individuals on that list and, in Brazil, to that total plus the number of votes for the list itself. The seats won by a list then are assigned to whichever individuals on the list received the most votes.

Japan's upper house (the Sangiin or House of Councillors) has 242 members, half elected every three years to a six-year term. Of the 242 members, 146 are elected by single non-transferable vote in 47 single- and multi-seat constituencies, and 96 are elected by nationwide open-list proportional representation (implemented by the D'Hondt rule). In electing those 96 members, voters cast a preference vote for one individual on a party list, and those preference votes determine the ranking of all individuals on the list.

Clearly, opening the list opens the door.

8.9 Parallel Voting (also known as "the Mixed-Member System")

8.9.1 How the System Selects the Winners

An election is held to fill two or more positions in a legislative chamber. Each voter receives two official ballots. The ballots may be either on separate sheets of paper or on separate parts of the same sheet.

One ballot is used to elect local representatives, usually by either single-winner or multi-winner plurality. Different districts will have different candidates and also may elect different numbers of representatives, so this ballot varies from district to district.

The second ballot is the same in every election district. It implements a closed-list or open-list election for all districts combined. However, individuals on the national list may simultaneously be local candidates.

There may be constraints on the lists and on one or both sets of winners. For example, in 2006, when half of the Palestinian Legislative Council was elected from geographical districts and half from closed lists, there were three different constraints. A list had to include at least one woman in the first three slots, at least one in the next four, and at least one in the five after that. To obtain a list seat, furthermore, a coalition needed to receive at least 2% of the total list vote. Also, six district seats were reserved for Christian candidates.

8.9.2 Numerical Example

In the 2006 Palestinian election, 66 individuals were elected from 16 districts by multi-winner plurality, while another 66 individuals were elected from 11 closed-party lists, using a 2% threshold and the Sainte-Laguë rule. Table 35 shows the results by faction.

To calculate Gallagher's index of disproportionality (I_D), we perform the following steps where S is the proportion of seats won and V is the proportion of votes received:

$$I_D = \sqrt{\frac{1}{2} \sum_{lists} (S - V)^2}$$

Table 35: 2006 Election of Palestinian Legislative Council by Parallel Voting

	Votes for List	Votes for List ÷Total List Vote	Seats Awarded by Sainte-Laguë Rule	Consti-tuency Seats Won	Total Seats Re-ceived	Total Seats Re-ceived ÷132	Total Seats Re-ceived per 100,000 Votes
Change and Reform (Hamas)	440,409	44.45%	29	45	74	56.06%	16.80
Liberation Movement of Palestine (Fatah)	410,554	41.43%	28	17	45	34.09%	10.96
Abu Ali Mustafa (PFLP)	42,101	4.25%	3	0	3	2.27%	7.13
The Alternative	28,973	2.92%	2	0	2	1.52%	6.90
Independent Palestine	26,909	2.72%	2	0	2	1.52%	7.43
Third Way	23,862	2.41%	2	0	2	1.52%	8.38
4 Other Lists	18,065	1.82%	0	0	0	0.00%	0.00
Independents	–	0.00%	0	4	4	3.03%	–
Total	990,873	100.00%	66	66	132	100.00%	13.32

$$\sum_{lists} (S - V)^2 = \left[\left(\frac{74}{132} - 0.4445 \right)^2 + \left(\frac{45}{132} - 0.4143 \right)^2 + \left(\frac{3}{132} - 0.0425 \right)^2 + \right.$$

$$\left(\frac{2}{132} - 0.0292 \right)^2 + \left(\frac{2}{132} - 0.0272 \right)^2 + \left(\frac{2}{132} - 0.0241 \right)^2 +$$

$$\left. \left(\frac{0}{132} - 0.0182 \right)^2 + \left(\frac{4}{132} - 0.0 \right)^2 \right]$$

$$\sum_{lists} (S - V)^2 = \left[(0.5606 - 0.4445)^2 + (0.3409 - 0.4143)^2 + (0.0227 - 0.0425)^2 + \right.$$

$$(0.0152 - 0.0292)^2 + (0.0152 - 0.0272)^2 + (0.0152 - 0.0241)^2 +$$

$$\left. (0.0 - 0.0182)^2 + (0.0303 - 0.0)^2 \right]$$

$$\sum_{lists} (S - V)^2 = \left[0.1161^2 + -0.0734^2 + -0.0198^2 + \right.$$

$$- 0.0140^2 + -0.0120^2 + 0.008948^2 +$$

$$\left. - 0.0182^2 + 0.0303^2 \right]$$

$$\sum_{lists} (S - V)^2 = 0.0135 + 0.0054 + 0.0004 + 0.0002 + 0.0001 + 0.0001 + 0.0067 + 0.0009$$

$$\sum_{lists} (S - V)^2 = 0.0273$$

$$I_D = \sqrt{0.5 \cdot 0.0273}$$
$$I_D = \sqrt{0.0136}$$
$$I_D = 0.1166$$

Note that Hamas received a minority of the list vote but obtained a majority of the 132 seats. That occurred because district representatives were elected by multi-winner plurality, not by a proportional system such as single transferable vote, with no offset in the allocation of list seats. Hamas won 45 (that is, 68%) of the 66 constituency seats although it received merely 44% of the list vote. In contrast, Fatah, which received 42% of the list vote, won merely 17 (that is, 26%) of the district seats — and those 17 include six seats in four districts (Bethlehem, Gaza, Jerusalem, and Ramallah) that were awarded to Christian candidates even if they were not among the leading vote-getters. Put differently, Hamas ended up with 17 seats per 100,000 list votes, while Fatah ended up with merely 11.

8.9.3 Who uses Parallel Voting

Parallel voting is used in electing part or all of the national legislature in Andorra, Armenia, Azerbaijan, Georgia, Guinea-Conakry, Japan, Kazakhstan, Korea, Lesotho, Lithuania, Mexico, Monaco, Nepal, Pakistan, Palestine, Philippines, Russia, Senegal, Seychelles, South Africa, Taiwan, Tajikistan, Thailand, Timor-Leste, Tunisia, and Ukraine.

The ratio of list seats to total seats varies widely. In recent years, it has been 19% in South Korea, 38% in Japan, 50% in Palestine, 69% in Armenia, and 90% in Timor-Leste.

8.10 Mixed-Member Proportional Representation (also known as MMP, "Personalized Proportional Representation", "the Additional-Member System", and "the German System")

8.10.1 Who uses Mixed-Member Proportional Representation

A dozen legislatures have MMP: (1) The "lower" house of the national legislature (Bundestag) and most state legislatures in Germany since 1949, (2) Denmark's unicameral Folketing since 1953, (3) Sweden's unicameral Rikstag since 1976, (4) Norway's unicameral Storting since 1989, (5) New Zealand's unicameral Parliament since 1996, (6) Scotland's unicameral Parliament, (7) Wales' unicameral National Assembly, (8) Venezuela's unicameral National Assembly since 1999, (9) London's Assembly since 2000, (10) Lesotho's National Assembly since 2002, (11) Bolivia's Chamber of Deputies since 2005, and (12) Romania's Senate and Chamber of Deputies since 2007.

New Zealand recently affirmed its choice. A referendum in November2011 asked, "Should New Zealand keep the Mixed Member Proportional (MMP) voting system?" There were 2,194,774 valid ballots, and 58% chose "Yes".

8.10.2 How the System Selects the Winners

A legislature with MMP, like a legislature chosen by parallel voting, has both local and national representatives. District tallies are used to fill some seats (called "constituency seats" or "district seats" or "permanent seats"), while a country-wide tally (or, in a provincial election, a state-wide tally) is used to allocate additional seats (called "adjustment seats" or "compensatory seats") to political parties. In allocating the adjustment seats, the objective is to make the total number of seats received by a party's candidates about the same as the proportion of the national vote received by the party, a feature lacking in parallel voting.

The number of adjustment seats varies widely. They constitute (a) 19 (11%) of a total of 150 seats in Norway, (b) 39 (11%) of a total of 349 seats in Sweden, (c) 39 (22%) of a total of 176 seats in Romania's Senate, (d) 40 (23%) of a total of 175 seats in Denmark,

(e) 50 (42%) of a normal total of 120 seats in New Zealand, and (f) 299 (50%) of a normal total of 598 seats in Germany.

Constituency seats are filled differently in different countries. Using a two-part ballot, like the ballot used with parallel voting, Germany and New Zealand elect district representatives by single-winner plurality. In contrast, voters in an election district in Denmark, Norway, or Sweden are offered a party list, and constituency seats are awarded to parties, Sweden having a 12% threshold in this connection.

Adjustment seats are everywhere awarded to political parties. Ideally, each political party receives no fewer — and no more — adjustment seats than are needed to make the sum of that party's constituency seats and adjustment seats be the proportion of the total seats in the legislature that, according to the country-wide party-list vote and, say, the Sainte-Laguë rule, that party should receive.

In fact, Germany and New Zealand do use the Sainte-Laguë rule when awarding adjustment seats. In contrast, when awarding both constituency and adjustment seats, Denmark uses the D'Hondt rule while both Norway and Sweden use the modified Sainte-Laguë rule.

However, there are thresholds. To qualify for adjustment seats in Norway or Sweden, a party must receive at least 4% of the national vote. In Denmark, a party must either receive at least 2% of the national vote or win at least one constituency seat . In New Zealand, a party must either receive at least 5% of the national vote or win at least one constituency seat. In Germany, a party must either receive at least 5% of the national vote or win at least 3 constituency seats.

Some party lists are closed and some are open. Germany and New Zealand award adjustment seats based on closed-list voting. In Denmark, Norway, and Sweden open party-lists are used to fill both constituency and adjustment seats. In Sweden, individuals move to the top of their party's list if they receive at least 8% of the party's votes in a constituency.

To achieve proportionality while honoring the constituency results, Germany and New Zealand — but not Denmark, Norway, or Sweden — will temporarily enlarge the legislature, awarding the additional seats (called "balance seats") to parties that won "too few" constituency seats. Currently, Germany's 598-seat Bundestag has 630 members, and New Zealand's 120-seat House of Representatives has 122 members.

At least in New Zealand, adjustment seats belong to parties, not to individuals. In 2004, at the request of the ACT Party, which had expelled the holder of an ACT list seat (Awatere Huata), New Zealand's Supreme Court awarded her seat to a candidate lower on ACT's list (Kenneth Wang) until the next election.

Consistent with party ownership of adjustment seats, surveys in several MMP countries indicate that national-list representatives spend more time than district representatives in party activities and with interest groups and, conversely, that district representatives spend more time than list representatives helping individual constituents in or from their districts.[16] For the U.S. House of Representatives, Markus Schulze has recommended a variation of the Scandinavian approach. In an email sent December 19th 2012 to electionscience@googlegroups.com, he recommended "Proportional representation by the single transferable vote on the district level with proportional compensation on the national level".

8.10.3 Numerical Example

Table 36: 2006 Election of Palestinian Legislative Council If MMP Had Been Used

	Votes for List	Votes for List ÷Total List Vote	Entitle-ment by Sainte-Laguë Rule[1]	Consti-tuency Seats Won	Adjust-ment Seats	Total Seats Re-ceived	Total Seats Re-ceived ÷132	Total Seats Re-ceived per 100,000 Votes
Change and Reform (Hamas)	440,409	44.45%	57	45	12	57	43.18%	12.9
Liberation Movement of Palestine (Fatah)	410,554	41.43%	54	17	37	54	40.91%	13.2
Abu Ali Mustafa (PFLP)	42,101	4.25%	6	0	6	6	4.55%	14.3
The Alternative	28,973	2.92%	4	0	4	4	3.03%	13.8
Independent Palestine	26,909	2.72%	4	0	4	4	3.03%	14.9
Third Way	23,862	2.41%	3	0	3	3	2.27%	12.6
4 Other Lists	18,065	1.82%	0	0	0	0	0.00%	0.0
Independents	–	0.00%	4	4	0	4	3.03%	–
Total	990,873	100.00%	132	66	66	132	100.00%	13.3

[1] 128th largest quotient is PFLP's $42,101 \div 11 = 3,827.4$

Recall that, In the 2006 election of the Palestinian Legislative Council, 66 individuals were elected from 16 districts by multi-winner plurality, while another 66 individuals were elected from 11 closed-party lists. Table 35 showed the results by faction. The outcome

---

[16]See (1) Matthew S. Shugart and Martin P. Wattenberg, eds., Mixed-Member Electoral Systems: The Best of Both Worlds? Oxford University Press, 2001, and (2) Robert G. Moser and Ethan Scheiner, Electoral Systems and Political Context: How the Effects of Rules Vary Across New and Established Democracies, Cambridge University Press, 2012.

of that election would have been very different if the 66 list seats had been allocated as adjustment seats, that is, if MMP had been used instead of parallel voting, Table 36 shows what the outcome would have been with MMP, given the same constituency results and the same 2% threshold, and Sainte-Laguë rule. In this table, Adjustment Seats is equivalent to the Entitlement less the Constituency Seats Won.

To calculate Gallagher's index of disproportionality (I_D), we perform the following steps where S is the proportion of seats won and V is the proportion of votes received:

$$I_D = \sqrt{\frac{1}{2} \sum_{lists} (S - V)^2}$$

$$\sum_{lists} (S - V)^2 = \left[\left(\frac{57}{132} - 0.4445 \right)^2 + \left(\frac{54}{132} - 0.4143 \right)^2 + \left(\frac{6}{132} - 0.0425 \right)^2 + \left(\frac{4}{132} - 0.0292 \right)^2 + \right.$$
$$\left. \left(\frac{4}{132} - 0.0272 \right)^2 + \left(\frac{3}{132} - 0.0241 \right)^2 + \left(\frac{0}{132} - 0.0182 \right)^2 + \left(\frac{4}{132} - 0.0 \right)^2 \right]$$

$$\sum_{lists} (S - V)^2 = \left[(0.4318 - 0.4445)^2 + (0.4091 - 0.4143)^2 + (0.04545 - 0.0425)^2 + (0.0303 - 0.0292)^2 + \right.$$
$$\left. (0.0303 - 0.0272)^2 + (0.02273 - 0.0241)^2 + (0.0 - 0.0182)^2 + (0.0303 - 0.0)^2 \right]$$

$$\sum_{lists} (S - V)^2 = \left[-0.127^2 + -0.0052^2 + 0.0030^2 + 0.0011^2 + -0.0031^2 + -0.0014^2 + \right.$$
$$\left. -0.0182^2 + 0.0303^2 \right]$$

$$\sum_{lists} (S - V)^2 = 0.00016 + 0.000027 + 0.000009 + 0.000001 + 0.00001 + 0.0000019 + 0.00033 + 0.00092$$

$$\sum_{lists} (S - V)^2 = 0.0014589$$

$$I_D = \sqrt{0.5 \cdot 0.0014589}$$
$$I_D = \sqrt{0.00072945}$$
$$I_D = 0.0270$$

Note that, with MMP, all factions receive about 13 seats per 100,000 votes while, with parallel voting, Hamas received about 17, Fatah received about 11, and the smaller factions received about 7. Similarly, the Gallagher index of disproportionality, which was 0.117 with parallel voting, now is merely 0.027 — a reduction of 77%!

8.10.4 Tactical Voting with MMP

Because a party winning constituency seats can qualify for adjustment seats in Germany and New Zealand even if it receives less than 5% of the party-list votes, some supporters of Germany's Christian Democratic Union and New Zealand's National Party cast their district votes for candidates affiliated with a small ally (the Free Democratic Party or the ACT Party). That explains why 20% of the district MPs elected in New Zealand in 2005 were not affiliated with the party that received a plurality of the party vote in their district.

Chapter 9

Which System is Best?

Table 2 above listed eight goals for a multi-winner election system. Table 37 shows how each of the ten multi-winner systems discussed in this section performs in each of these eight respects.

Table 37 is disappointing. It indicates that no multi-winner election system dominates. That is, for none of the systems does a paired comparison with each of the other systems indicate that that system is more desirable in some respects and no less desirable in the other respects. Hence, even if you agree with the eight goals listed in the table, you cannot identify a best system unless you compare the advantages and disadvantages of each system, and that is both difficult and subjective.

If you favor a minority party or cause, then you probably will advocate closed-list voting. Closed-list voting fosters party discipline and ideological purity, and the threshold to qualify for seats in the legislature can be quite low (2% of the total vote is not unusual). In addition, you might choose the Sainte-Laguë rule , which is more favorable to small parties than either the D'Hondt rule or the modified Sainte-Laguë rule.

On the other hand, if you want to increase voters' freedom of choice, then you might prefer open-list voting. With open-list voting, voters can move individual candidates to the top of a party's list, and the rules can make moving up as easy or difficult as you wish. Both closed-list voting and open-list voting produce rough proportionality for the political parties, and proportionality tends to increase if the whole country is one election district, the number of seats in the legislature is increased, and small parties can form alliances.

If you want local representatives in addition to statewide or national representatives, then consider mixed-member proportional representation. You can add local representatives to either closed-list or open-list voting for national representatives. Any single-winner or multi-winner system can be used to elect the local representatives, the possibilities ranging from simple plurality (as in Germany) to open-list district elections (as in Sweden). Electing local representatives by simple plurality does foster gerrymandering and tactical voting, but, with MMP, unlike parallel voting, the national seats are adjustment seats, and

Table 37: The Multi-Winner Election Systems Reviewed Below

	Multi-Winner Plurality	Limited Voting	Cumulative Voting	Single Transferable Vote	Multiple Transferable Vote	Constrained STV	Closed Lists	Open Lists	Parallel Voting	Mixed Member Proportional
Proportional[1]	No	No	Yes	Yes	No	Yes	Yes	Yes	No	Yes
Monotonic[2]	Yes	Yes	No	No	Yes	Yes	Yes	Yes	Yes	Yes
Voters Sovereign[3]	Yes	Yes	Yes	Yes	Yes	No	No	No	No	Yes
Automatic Allocation[4]	No	No	No	No	No	No	Yes	No	No	No
Independent of Clones[5]	No	No	No	Yes	Yes	Yes	I*	I*	I*	No
Sincere Voting[6]	Fair	Fair	Fine	Fine	Fine	Fine	Good	Fine	Good	Good
Transparent[7]	Good	Good	Fair	Fair	Fair	Fair	Fine	Good	Good	Good
Verifiable[8]	Yes	Yes	Yes	No	No	No	Yes	Yes	Yes	Yes

* Incomplete

1 The proportion of open seats won by candidates favored by a faction of the voters and disfavored by other voters is as close to the proportion of votes cast by that faction as is possible, given that, when n seats are open, the fraction won must be $\frac{0}{n}, \frac{1}{n}, \frac{2}{n}, \dots,$ or $\frac{n}{n}$.

2 Elevating the rank that a voter assigns to a particular candidate, while making no change in the order of other candidates, will not deprive that candidate of victory.

3 Voters choose or rank individual candidates, not just lists of candidates.

4 Votes are automatically apportioned among candidates as the voters casting those votes would wish if they knew which candidates needed additional support.

5 Suppose that two candidates are so alike that no voter would rank any other candidate between them. Then, if each of the two would be elected provided the other were not a candidate, one of the two will be elected if both are candidates. And, if each would lose provided the other were not a candidate, then each will lose if the other is a candidate.

6 It is likely that voters will report their true preferences.

7 It is easy for voters to understand how the outcome will be determined.

8 The outcome can be confirmed simply by re-tallying ballots and re-adding subtotals.

awarding them lessens the effect of biased districts and insincere voting.

There are, however, reasons to reject list voting. You may want voters to be free to vote for individuals nominated by more than one political party, and you may distrust party leaders or worry about corruption. If so, you might opt for the single transferable vote or its twin, that is, the multiple transferable vote. Like open-list and closed-list voting, those systems give proportional representation to different factions. They also maximize voter sovereignty — but, if you want restrictions on the outcome, such as seats reserved for an ethnic group or gender, such curbs can be added, producing constrained STV or constrained MTV.

You may like STV or MTV but think that it would be difficult to verify the absence of fraud and errors, or it would be inordinately expensive to prepare, certify, and install the software. If so, consider limited voting and cumulative voting. While those systems, unlike STV and MTV, do not avoid disproportionality, at least they do not, like multi-winner plurality, allow a bare majority — and even a minority — of voters to choose all of the winners.

Since no multi-winner election system is dominant, there is no demonstrably correct answer to the title question.

Part III

More About the Single Transferable Vote

Chapter 10

Versions of STV

Different users implement STV differently. There are important differences in five respects, as follows:

1. How many candidates a voter may or must rank,

2. Whether the quota is adjusted as ballots are exhausted,

3. The initial value of the quota,

4. Whether voters' rankings are processed manually or by computer, and

5. When voters' rankings are processed, (a) do votes not transfer from a newly-elected or newly-eliminated candidate (i) both to candidates who were eliminated and candidates who were elected at earlier stages of the calculations, or (ii) only to candidates who were eliminated at earlier stages, (b) do votes transfer from a newly-elected candidate to the next available choice (i) on any ballot that gave a vote to that newly-elected candidate, or (ii) only on a ballot in the batch of ballots whose transfer put the newly-elected candidate over the top, and (c) does (i) a fraction of a vote transfer from a newly-elected candidate to all eligible recipients, or (ii) a whole vote transfer to a randomly-selected subset of the eligible recipients.

We will discuss these issues in turn.

10.1 Constraints on the Number of Candidates That a Voter May or Must Rank

In an STV election outside of Australia, a voter may rank as few candidates as the voter wishes. That rule (which Australians call "optional preferential voting") also applies in the STV elections of the unicameral legislature of Queensland — but not in other STV elections in Australia.

A rule called "Partial Preferential Voting" applies In the STV elections of both the "lower" house (House of Assembly) of Tasmania and the unicameral legislature of Australian Capital Territory. There, a ballot is valid only if the voter ranks at least as many candidates as will be elected.

And a rule called "full preferential voting with optional above-the-line voting" applies in both the STV elections of Australia's national Senate and the STV elections of the "upper" houses (Legislative Councils) of New South Wales, South Australia, Victoria, and Western Australia. With this rule, each political party prepares a list of candidates ("group-voting ticket") and designates which other parties' lists should be appended if and when the last of its own candidates is eliminated. In turn, a voter's ballot is valid only if the voter either chooses a party list or ranks every single candidate.

10.2   Adjustment of the Quota

In New Zealand, the quota decreases as ballots are exhausted. Elsewhere, the quota does not change, but candidate(s) are allowed to fill the last seat(s) without reaching the quota. For example, a publication of the government of Ireland says, "[If] there are three continuing candidates, two unfilled seats and [either no available surplus or available surplus too small to raise the lowest candidate to or above the second lowest candidate, then the] lowest continuing candidate is excluded and the remaining two candidates are deemed elected to fill the last seats."[1]

10.3   Initial Value of the Quota

Australia, Cambridge, MA Malta, Northern Ireland, and Republic of Ireland set the quota at the integer above the numerical value of $\frac{B}{1+O}$ where B is the number of valid ballots and O is the number of openings. A candidate receiving at least that many votes is elected.

To illustrate, Malta's Elections Act says that (a) the quota is the total number of valid votes cast, divided by the number of seats to be filled increased by one and adding one to the result, disregarding any decimal remainder, and (b) If at the end of any count, the number of votes credited to a candidate is equal to or greater than the quota, the candidate shall thereupon be elected.[2] For example, if six seats are open and the number of votes cast is at least 700 and at most 706, then 101 is both the quota and the minimum number of votes that is sufficient for election.

---

[1] Republic of Ireland, Guide to Ireland's PR-STV Electoral System, 2011.

[2] Republic of Malta, General Elections Act, Article 105.

In contrast, in New Zealand the value of the quota at any stage is $\frac{B}{1+O}$ where B is the number of non-exhausted ballots and O is the original number of openings, truncated (without rounding) at nine decimal places and then increased by $0.000\,000\,001$. A candidate having at least that many votes at any stage of the calculations is elected. At the first tally, the number of votes for a candidate is an integer and no ballots have yet been exhausted, so the formula used in New Zealand will produce the same winners as the formula used elsewhere until some ballots have been exhausted.

10.4 Computerization

Some users capture voters' rankings by data entry, optical scanner, memory card, direct recording, and/or online voting and upload the rankings to a computer. The computer separates multi-election data by contest and then, for each contest, calculates the quota, processes voters' rankings, and determines the winners. Other users process voters' rankings manually.

In 2002, the Republic of Ireland began preparing for electronic elections. Several years later, a Commission on Electronic Voting reported that the software had mistakes, printouts for post-audits and recounts were not available, voting by disabled individuals was not secret — and that correcting these deficiencies would be inordinately costly. In 2009, accordingly, the government sold the direct-recording voting machines it had acquired, recommitted to manual processing of paper ballots, and reconciled itself to taking several days — and even longer when there is a recount — to determine the winners.

Similarly, the Republic of Malta processes voters' ranking manually.

In Cambridge, MA, work that, before 1997, took 100 hand-workers six days to complete is now done by a computer in less than three minutes on election night. Voting Solutions LLC, a partnership based in Oakland, CA, developed the program, which it named ChoicePlus Pro 2.1.[3]

Many student governments — for example, the Associated Students of the University of California, in 2002 — also have adopted ChoicePlus Pro 2.1. Unlike Cambridge, however, they transfer a newly-elected candidate's surplus in fractions of a vote. That, in fact, is the default version of the program.

In Australia, programs developed by Software Improvements, a company based in Canberra, have been used since 1998. Before 1998, it took up to three weeks to announce the winners.

In New Zealand, a program developed by electionz.com, a company based in Aukland, has been used since 2004.

Currently, five U.S. companies are developing election software, namely, Dominion, Election Systems & Software, Hart Intercivic, TrueBallot, and Unisyn. However, none

---

[3]For stage-by-stage details of a recent Cambridge, MA election — it had 17 stages — see `http://rwinters.com/elections/council2013.pdf`.

seems to be close to offering a certifiable version of STV — or even of full IRV.

10.5   Transfer of Votes

Different users have different rules concerning how votes are redistributed when a candidate is elected or eliminated. In particular, users differ with respect to (a) whether votes can transfer from a newly-elected or newly-eliminated candidate to candidates who were elected at an earlier stage of the calculations, (b) whether votes can transfer from a newly-elected candidate only to candidates who are the next-lower choices on one of the ballots that put the newly-elected candidate over the top (the "last parcel method"), and (c) whether a fraction of a vote transfers from a newly elected candidate to all eligible recipients ("the Gregory rule") or a whole vote transfers to a randomly-selected subset of the eligible recipients. Here is a user-by-user summary.

10.5.1   Republic of Ireland

When a candidate has more votes than needed for election, officials divide the last-received batch of ballots, that is, the ballots that brought that candidate above the quota, into those that are "transferable", that is, have a lower choice who is a continuing candidate, and those that are not, and then physically move as many of those transferable ballots as there are above-quota votes. The ballots given to each continuing candidate are selected at random from all ballots in the last-received batch on which that candidate is the next lower choice, and the proportion of all ballots being moved that each continuing candidate receives is approximately equal to the proportion of the last-received transferable ballots on which that candidate is the next lower choice.

A government publication provides a numerical illustration: "[I]f Abe was 6 votes short of the quota and then got 10 votes in a particular count, he/she would have a surplus of 4 votes. The 10 votes that got him/her elected are examined and 8 are found to be transferable, viz. 6 to Cal and 2 to Dee. The ratio of the surplus of 4 votes to the 8 transferable papers in Abe's last parcel) of votes is 0.5. This ratio is applied to the sub-parcels) of next preferences for Cal and Dee. Thus, the votes transferred in the distribution of Abe's surplus of 4 votes are the top three votes in the sub-parcel of next preferences for Cal, together with the top vote in the sub-parcel of next preferences for Dee."[4]

What happens if a candidate who receives one of the ballots being moved is eliminated at a later stage of the calculations? Then, if that ballot has yet another next choice and is again, by chance, chosen for transfer, the ballot again gives a whole vote to the candidate who receives it.

---

[4]Republic of Ireland, Guide to Ireland's PR-STV Electoral System, 2011.

10.5.2   Republic of Malta

As in Ireland, when a candidate has more votes than needed for election, officials in Malta divide the last-received batch of ballots into those that are "transferable" and those that are not. Then, however, officials determine, to four decimal places, the ratio of the number of above-quota votes being transferred to the number of transferable ballots, write that fraction on each transferable ballot, and put each transferable ballot in the pile of the continuing candidate who is next choice on that ballot. If the candidate who receives one of those ballots is eliminated at a later stage of the calculations, and if that ballot has yet another next choice, then that ballot gives the same fraction of a vote to its next recipient.

10.5.3   Cambridge, Massachusetts

ChoicePlus Pro 2.1 allows transfer of a newly-elected candidate's above-quota votes deterministically and in fractions of a vote, but Cambridge has chosen an optional version that — as in Ireland — transfers above-quota votes semi-randomly and as whole votes.

For example, if ⅓ of the votes of a newly-elected candidate should be transferred, then the ballots providing those votes are, in effect, re-numbered and a whole vote moves to the next choice on ballot #3, on ballot #6, on ballot #9, etc. (except that (a) if a duplicate ranking causes more than one candidate to be the next choice on a ballot, then the vote goes to the next continuing candidate whose rank is not duplicated, and (b) a different ballot is chosen whenever (i) one of the numbered ballots no longer ranks a continuing candidate, or (ii) the transferee would be receiving more votes than needed for election). A noteworthy consequence is that changing the numbers assigned to the ballots might change the outcome.

10.5.4   Australia

Australia has three different protocols concerning transfer of above-quota votes. One procedure (the "last parcel method") applies when electing the House of Assembly of Tasmania and the Legislative Assembly of Australian Capital Territory. A second procedure (transferring whole votes to a random selection of all continuing candidates) applies when electing the Legislative Council of New South Wales. The third procedure applies when electing the national Senate and the Legislative Councils of South Australia, Victoria and Western Australia. Let's focus on the third procedure.

When a newly-elected candidate has more votes than needed for election, the computer determines, to six decimal places, the ratio of above-quota votes to total votes for that candidate. For each other continuing candidate, the computer then (a) multiplies that ratio (called the "transfer value") by the sum, over all ballots giving a whole or fractional vote (the latter exist after the first seat is filled) to the newly-elected candidate on which that other continuing candidate is next choice, of the whole or fractional vote that originated on each such ballot, and (b) adds that product, rounded down to the nearest integer, to the tally of that other continuing candidate.

If a continuing candidate to whom above-quota votes were transferred is eliminated at a later stage of the calculations, then those transferred votes, multiplied by the associated transfer value, transfer to whichever other continuing candidate is the following choice on the ballots where those votes originated. On the other hand, if the transferee is elected at a later stage, then those transferred votes, multiplied by both the associated transfer value and a transfer value for the newly-elected candidate, transfer to whichever continuing candidate is the following choice on the ballots where the votes originated. The process continues until all seats have been filled.[5]

10.5.5 New Zealand

New Zealand's STV software does something that is not — perhaps not yet — done elsewhere, something that minimizes the effect both of chance and of the order in which candidates are elected or eliminated. Uniquely, New Zealand's program transfers votes, not only to continuing candidates, but also to already-elected candidates – and then immediately again transfers above-quota votes from the already-elected candidates to their supporters' next choices.

This procedure gives ballots on which a particular candidate is ranked first the same weight as ballots on which that candidate becomes top choice after another candidate is eliminated. As a result, the order in which already-elected candidates were elected does not affect how many votes each continuing candidate has — and therefore does not affect which continuing candidate will be elected next.

When transferring votes, the computer uses a set of variables called "keep values." A candidate's current keep value is (a) 0 for an eliminated candidate, (b) 1 both for a continuing (that is, neither eliminated nor elected) candidate and for an exhausted ballot, and (c) for an already-elected candidate, the ratio of the current quota to that candidate's current tally.

From a ballot on which a candidate is ranked m^{th}, that candidate receives a fraction of a vote, equal to $(1 - k_1) \cdot (1 - k_2) \cdot \ldots \cdot (1 - k_{m-1}) \cdot k_m$, where $k_1, k_2, \ldots k_m$ denote the current keep value of the candidates ranked, respectively, first, second, $\ldots$ and m^{th} on that ballot. This formula implies that, at each tally, (a) an eliminated candidate receives 0 from every ballot; (b) a continuing candidate receives (i) a whole vote from every ballot on which all higher-ranked candidates have been eliminated, (ii) 0 from every ballot on which at least one other continuing candidate is ranked higher, and (iii) a fraction of a vote from every ballot on which all higher-ranked candidates have been elected; and (c) an already-elected candidate receives votes as if still a continuing candidate, but scaled down to make the elected candidate's current tally equal the current value of the quota.

---

[5]For details of an actual election — it had 175 stages! — see http://www.abc.net.au/elections/federal/2004/results/sendQLD.htm

The computer rounds each fraction that it transfers. Specifically, the computer rounds each fraction up at the ninth decimal place and, accordingly, determines candidates' tallies to the ninth decimal place.[6]

Brian Meek, an English mathematician, created this version of STV in 1969.[7] It became usable 18 years later, when three other English mathematicians showed that the simultaneous equations that were involved could be solved by successive approximation.[8]

One the authors of the 1987 paper later compared outcomes with Meek STV with outcomes with a less advanced version of STV. Using data for 188 elections, most with three-seven open seats, he found that there would have been one or two different winners in 19 cases. He concluded, "[U]nless it is essential to have a manual, witnessed count, the Meek rules should be used for STV counting. The approximations introduced to enable a manual count produce too many differences . . ."[9]

---

[6]New Zealand Department of Internal Affairs, Meek's method, 2014, http://www.dia.govt.nz/DIAWebsite.nsf/0/38f781eae0881449cc256c0f00152ea3?OpenDocument.

[7]B. Meek, "A new approach to the single transferable vote," Mathématiques et Sciences Humaines, 1969.

[8]I. D. Hill, B. A. Wichmann and D. R. Woodall. "Algorithm 123 — single transferable vote by Meek's method," Computer Journal (UK), 30:277-281, 1987.

[9]Brian A. Wichmann, "Do the Differences Matter?" Voting Matters, 14:4-5, 2001.

Chapter 11

Numerical Example of Meek's Method

Five individuals, namely, Abe, Ben, Cal, Dee, and Eve, are eligible for three open seats; 80 voters submit a valid ballot; and the ballots have the rankings shown in Table 38.

Table 38: Rankings Used in Meek Example

Rankings of Candidates	Number of Ballots with That Ranking:
Abe	4
Abe >Ben	2
Abe >Ben >Cal	32
Ben	3
Ben >Abe >Cal >Dee	8
Cal >Dee >Ben >Abe >Eve	6
Dee >Eve >Cal	16
Eve >Dee	9
Total	80

Step 1: (a) Determine the initial quota Q_1, that is, the largest number of votes that is not quite large enough to be elected on the first tally. The formula (usually mislabeled "the Droop quota") is

$$Q_1 = \frac{B}{O + 1}$$

where B is the number of valid ballots and O is number of openings.

$$Q_1 = \frac{80}{3+1} = 20$$

(b) For each candidate, determine the initial tally, that is, number of votes initially held by that candidate. It equals the number of valid ballots on which that candidate is first choice.

Letting $V(\text{Abe}, 1)$ denote the number of votes initially held by Abe, $V(\text{Ben}, 1)$ denote the number of votes initially held by Ben, etc., the rankings imply the following tallies:

$$V(\text{Abe}, 1) = 38$$
$$V(\text{Ben}, 1) = 11$$
$$V(\text{Cal}, 1) = 6$$
$$V(\text{Dee}, 1) = 16$$
$$V(\text{Eve}, 1) = 9$$
$$\text{Total} = 80$$

(c) Any candidate whose first tally is greater than Q_1 is elected on the first tally.

Because $V(\text{Abe}, 1) > Q_1$, while $V(\text{Ben}, 1)$, $V(\text{Cal}, 1)$, $V(\text{Dee}, 1)$, and $V(\text{Eve}, 1) \leq Q_1$, Abe — and only Abe — is elected on the first tally.

Comment: If all openings had been filled at Step 1c, then the election would be complete. Conversely, if no candidate had been elected at Step 1c, then we would jump to Step 4a below, that is, begin eliminating candidates. In our example, however, a candidate was elected at Step 1c and more seats are open, so we proceed to Step 2a.

Step 2: (a) For each candidate elected on the first tally, determine how many of the ballots that rank that candidate first are "exhausted", that is, have no next choice.

Four ballots ranking Abe first have no second choice.

(b) For each elected candidate, write equations that express the relation between (i) the second quota Q_2, that is, the largest number of votes that is not quite large enough to be elected on the second tally, and (ii) that candidate's "keep value", that is, the proportion of that candidate's votes that that candidate needs to retain — instead of transferring to supporters' second choices — in order to have a tally equal to the second quota.

If we let a_2 denote the proportion of $V(\text{Abe}, 1)$, that is, of Abe's first tally, that Abe must retain in order to have $V(\text{Abe}, 2)$, that is, Abe's second tally, equal to Q_2, then we have the following pair of equations:

$$Q_2 = \frac{80 - (4 \cdot (1 - a2))}{3 + 1}$$

$$Q_2 = V(\text{Abe}, 2) = a_2 \cdot V(\text{Abe}, 1) = a_2 \cdot 38$$

(c) Solve those equations (a) for the current value of the keep value of each already-elected candidate, and (b) for Q_2.

$$a_2 = \frac{19}{37} = 0.5135$$

$$Q_2 = \frac{722}{37} = 19.5135$$

(d) Examine the ballots that ranked an elected candidate first and note (a) how many ranked each other candidate second, and (b) how many had no second choice.

38 valid ballots ranked Abe first. Of those ballots, 34 ranked Ben second while the other four have no second choice.

(e) For each candidate ranked second on at least one ballot that ranked an elected candidate first, determine the second tally. The latter will include surplus transferred from the elected candidate.

$$V(\text{Ben}, 2) = V(\text{Ben}, 1) + (2 + 32) \cdot (1 - a_2)$$

$$= 11 + 34 \cdot \left(1 - \frac{19}{37}\right)$$

$$= 27.5405$$

(f) Determine the number of votes that — because some ballots have no next choice — do not transfer from a candidate elected on the first tally to any other candidate. These nontransferable votes reduce the quota, so the next step is to determine their current number (which will be denoted L_2, meaning leakage at Step 2).

$$L_2 = 4 \cdot (1 - a_2)$$

$$= 4 \cdot \left(1 - \frac{19}{37}\right)$$

$$= 1.9459$$

(g) Set the tally of each elected candidate equal to Q_2, and confirm that the total vote-count still equals the number of valid ballots.

$$V(\text{Abe}, 2) = 19.5135$$
$$V(\text{Ben}, 2) = 27.5405$$
$$V(\text{Cal}, 2) = 6$$
$$V(\text{Dee}, 2) = 16$$
$$V(\text{Eve}, 2) = 9$$
$$L_2 = 1.9459$$
$$\text{Total} = 80$$

(h) Any candidate whose second tally is greater than Q_2 is elected on the second tally.

Because $V(\text{Ben}, 2) > Q_2$, while $V(\text{Cal}, 2)$, $V(\text{Dee}, 2)$, and $V(\text{Eve}, 2) \leq Q_2$, Ben — and only Ben — is elected on the second tally.

Comment: If the last opening had been filled at Step 2h, then the election would be complete. Conversely, if no candidate had been elected at Step 2h, then we would jump to Step 4a below, that is, begin eliminating unelected candidates. In our example, however, at least one candidate was elected at Step 2h and at least one seat is still open, so we proceed to Step 3a.

Step 3: (a) To obtain current values for leakage, quota, and tallies, identify feedback to already-elected candidates.

Eight ballots ranking Ben first rank Abe second. As a result, $8 \cdot (1 - b_3)$ votes will transfer from Ben to Abe, and Abe will keep $a_3 \cdot 8 \cdot (1 - b_3)$ of that transfer, where a_3 and b_3 denote, respectively, the proportion of Abe's or Ben's votes that that candidate needs to retain in order to have a tally equal to the third quota Q_3.

(b) Also identify additional exhausted ballots.

Three ballots ranking Ben first have no second choice. Lack of a second choice on these ballots, like lack of a second choice on four ballots ranking Abe first, increases L_3 and reduces Q_3. In particular, L_3 will include $3 \cdot (1 - b_3)$.

$$Q_3 = \frac{80 - (4 \cdot (1 - a_3)) - (2 \cdot (1 - a_3) \cdot (1 - b_3)) - (3 \cdot (1 - b_3))}{3 + 1}$$
$$Q_3 = V(\text{Abe}, 3) = (a_3 \cdot 38) + (a_3 \cdot 8 \cdot (1 - b_3))$$
$$Q_3 = V(\text{Ben}, 3) = (b_3 \cdot 11) + (b_3 \cdot 34 \cdot (1 - a_3))$$

(c) Solve those three equations for Q_3, a_3, and b_3. The answers are as follows:

$$a_3 = 0.469484$$
$$b_3 = 0.658556$$
$$Q_3 = 19.122830$$

Comment: For elected-candidates Abe and Ben, the next tallies, that is, $V(\text{Abe}, 3)$ and $V(\text{Ben}, 3)$, will be set equal to Q_3, that is, to 19.122830. In turn, the keep values a_3 and b_3 will be used to determine both L_3, that is, the new value of the leakage, and the number of votes transferred to candidates who, on at least one ballot, were out-ranked only by Abe and Ben.

(d) Determine the number of votes that — because some ballots have no second or third choice — transfer from a candidate elected on the first or second tally, not to another candidate, but instead to the hypothetical bucket (L_3). These votes reduce the quota.

$$\begin{aligned} L_3 &= 4 \cdot (1 - a_3) + 2 \cdot (1 - a_3) \cdot (1 - b_3) + 3 \cdot (1 - b_3) \\ &= 4 \cdot (1 - 0.469484) + 2 \cdot (1 - 0.469484) \cdot (1 - 0.658556) + 3 \cdot (1 - 0.658556) \\ &= 3.5087 \end{aligned}$$

(e) Now identify candidates who, on at least one ballot, were out-ranked only by already-elected candidates.

Thirty-two ballots ranking Abe first and Ben second rank Cal third. As a result, $(1 - b_3) \cdot 32 \cdot (1 - a_3)$ votes that initially were included in $V(\text{Abe}, 1)$ will become part of $V(\text{Cal}, 3)$.

(f) For each candidate who, on at least one ballot, was out-ranked only by already-elected candidates, determine the third tally. The latter will include surplus transferred from the already-elected candidates.

$$\begin{aligned} V(\text{Cal}, 3) &= 6 + 32 \cdot (1 - a_3) \cdot (1 - b_3) + 8 \cdot (1 - b_3) \cdot (1 - a_3) \\ &= 6 + 32 \cdot (1 - 0.469484) \cdot (1 - 0.65855) + 8 \cdot (1 - 0.65855) \cdot (1 - 0.469484) \\ &= 13.2457 \end{aligned}$$

(g) Set the tally of elected candidates equal to Q_3, and confirm that the total vote-count, including leakage, still equals the number of valid ballots.

$$V(\text{Abe}, 3) = 19.1228$$
$$V(\text{Ben}, 3) = 19.1228$$
$$V(\text{Cal}, 3) = 13.2457$$
$$V(\text{Dee}, 3) = 16$$
$$V(\text{Eve}, 3) = 9$$
$$L_3 = 3.5087$$
$$\text{Total} = 80$$

(h) Any candidate whose third tally is greater than Q_3 is elected on the third tally.

Because $V(\text{Cal}, 3) \leq Q_3$, $V(\text{Dee}, 3) \leq Q_3$, and $V(\text{Eve}, 3) \leq Q_3$, no additional candidates are elected on the third tally.

Comment: If the last open seat had been filled at Step 3h, then the election would be complete. Conversely, if at least one seat had been filled at Step 3h but at least one other seat was still open, then we would repeat Steps 3a–3h — that is, transfer surplus from elected candidates to other candidates — until either the last opening was filled or no additional candidates were elected. In our example, however, no candidate was elected at Step 3h and one seat is still open, so we proceed to Step 4a.

Step 4:   (a) Eliminate from contention whichever candidate has the fewest votes (breaking any ties randomly).

Because $V(\text{Eve}, 3) < V(\text{Cal}, 3) < V(\text{Dee}, 3)$, Eve is eliminated.

(b) On every ballot that ranked the eliminated candidate above at least one other candidate, remove the eliminated candidate and raise the rank of lower-ranked candidates accordingly.

Eliminating Eve alters rankings on 9 ballots on which Eve was first choice and 16 ballots where Eve was second choice. On the 9 ballots where Eve was first, Dee rises from second choice to first. On the 16 ballots where Eve was second, Cal rises from third to second.

(c) Identify both newly-exhausted ballots and feedback to already-elected candidates. Either will change leakage, quota, and keep values.

Eve received votes only from the 9 ballots where Eve was first choice. There is a next choice on each of those ballots, and that next choice is neither Abe or Ben. Hence, eliminating Eve does not exhaust any additional ballots or change Abe's or Ben's keep value. As a result, neither the leakage nor the quota changes. That is, $L_4 = L_3 = 3.5087$, and $Q_4 = Q_3 = 19.1228$.

(d) Redetermine the tallies. The tally of an eliminated candidate goes to 0 and stays there, while the tally of an already-elected candidate continues to equal the quota (however, if eliminating a candidate exhausts more ballots or transfers votes to an already-elected candidate, both the quota and an elected candidate's tally will decrease).

Because Dee is second choice on each of the 9 ballots from which Eve received votes, eliminating Eve causes all of Eve's 9 votes to transfer to Dee. Consequently, the new tallies are as follows:

$$V(\text{Abe}, 4) = 19.1228$$
$$V(\text{Ben}, 4) = 19.1228$$
$$V(\text{Cal}, 4) = 13.2457$$
$$V(\text{Dee}, 4) = 16 + 9 = 25$$
$$V(\text{Eve}, 4) = 0$$
$$L_4 = 3.5087$$
$$\text{Total} = 80$$

(e) Any candidate whose fourth tally is greater than or equal to Q_4 is elected on the fourth tally.

Because $V(\text{Dee}, 4) \geq Q_4$, Dee is elected on the fourth tally.

Comment: If no seat had been filled at Step 4e, then we would repeat Steps 4a–4e (that is, eliminate other candidates) until at least one seat was filled. Then, if at least one seat was still open, we would repeat Step 3a–3h (that is, again transfer surplus from elected candidates) until either the last opening was filled or no additional candidates were elected — and then repeat Steps 4a–4e. In our example, however, the last open seat was filled at Step 4e, so this election is complete. The winners are Abe, Ben, and Dee.

Note that 49 (61%) of the 80 voters ranked Abe and Ben either first or second and that Abe and Ben win 67% of the open seats. Conversely, 25 (31%) of the voters ranked Dee (along with Eve) either first or second, and Dee wins 33% of the open seats. That is as close to proportionality as is possible when three indivisible individuals will win three indivisible seats and voters have the indicated rankings.

Note, too, that, while the quota for election, even after leakage, was always greater than 19 votes, Ben and Dee were elected despite being the first choice of merely 11 and 16 voters, respectively. When Abe was elected, STV automatically transferred Abe's surplus votes to whichever candidate was ranked second on the ballots where Abe's votes originated — and that was Ben. Similarly, when Eve was eliminated, STV automatically transferred all of Eve's votes to whichever candidate was ranked second on the ballots where Eve's votes originated — and that was Dee. Those transfers produced the proportionality, and proportionality would be even more evident if there were more than three open seats.

Chapter 12

Tactical Voting with STV

STV — and therefore MTV — invites a tactic called "Woodall free riding." This involves ranking a hopeless candidate first, ranking your real top choice second, and ranking your real second choice third. With a version of STV that does not transfer votes to already-elected candidates, ranking candidates in that order will help your real second choice whenever your real first choice is elected before the hopeless candidate is eliminated. With Meek's method, however, the tactic has no reward.

A two-part example should clarify both why free riding works with a pre-Meek version of STV and why Meek's method nullifies the gain.

Suppose that there are three open seats, five candidates (namely, Abe, Ben, Cal, Dee, and Eve), and the 400 rankings shown in Table 39a.

Table 39a: Rankings Used to Illustrate Tactics with STV

Rankings of Candidates	Number of Voters with that Ranking:
Abe >Cal	50
Abe >Dee >Ben	105
Ben	90
Cal >Ben	80
Dee >Ben	75

With sincere voting, all versions of STV elect Abe at Stage 1, Dee at Stage 2, and Ben at Stage 3. Table 39b shows the calculations.

Table 39b: Outcome with Sincere Voting

	Stage			
	1	2	3	4
Exhausted Ballots	0	0	0	0
Quota	$400 \cdot \frac{1}{3+1}$ $= 100.0$	$400 \cdot \frac{1}{3+1}$ $= 100.0$	$400 \cdot \frac{1}{3+1}$ $= 100.0$	$400 \cdot \frac{1}{3+1}$ $= 100.0$
Votes for Abe	155.0	100.0	100.0	100.0
Votes for Ben	90.0	90.0	102.3	100.0
Votes for Cal	80.0	97.7	97.7	–
Votes for Dee	75.0	112.3	100.0	100.0
Votes for Eve	0.0	0.0	0.0	–
Votes not transferable	0.0	0.0	0.0	100.0
Total votes	400	400	400	400

Stage:

1: Because Abe has both more than a quota of votes and more votes than any other candidate, elect Abe; also, transfer Abe's surplus, i.e. $105 + 50 - 100.0 = 55.0$ votes, to the next choice(s) on the 155 ballots where Abe was first choice, i.e. to Cal and Dee, and set Abe's tally at the quota, that is, at 100.0. Of Abe's surplus, Cal receives receives $50 \cdot \frac{55}{155} = 17.7$ votes and Dee receives $105 \cdot \frac{55}{155} = 37.3$.

2: Because Dee now has both more than a quota of votes and more votes than any other candidate, elect Dee; also, transfer Dee's surplus, i.e. $112.3 - 100.0 = 12.3$ votes, to the next choice(s) on the $105 + 75 = 180$ ballots where Dee was top choice, i.e. to Ben, and set Dee's tally at the quota, that is, at 100.0.

3: Because Ben has both more than a quota of votes and more votes than any other candidate, elect Ben and set Ben's tally at the quota, that is, at 100.0.

4: Crown Abe, Ben and Dee.

To calculate the index of disproportionality for four factions when Abe, Ben and Dee win, we perform the following steps where S is the proportion of seats received and V is the proportion of votes received:

$$= \sqrt{\frac{1}{2} \sum_{factions} (S-V)^2}$$

$$= \sqrt{\frac{1}{2}\left(\left(\frac{1}{3} - \frac{155}{400}\right)^2 + \left(\frac{1}{3} - \frac{90}{400}\right)^2 + \left(\frac{0}{3} - \frac{90}{400}\right)^2 + \left(\frac{1}{3} - \frac{75}{400}\right)^2\right)}$$

$$= \sqrt{\frac{1}{2}\left((0.3333 - 0.3875)^2 + (0.3333 - 0.225)^2 + (0.0 - 0.2)^2 + (0.3333 - 0.1875)^2\right)}$$

$$= \sqrt{\frac{1}{2}\left(-0.54167^2 + 0.108333^2 + -0.2^2 + 0.1458^2\right)}$$

$$= \sqrt{\frac{1}{2}\left(0.002934 + 0.0117361 + 0.04 + 0.02125764\right)}$$

$$= \sqrt{0.5 \cdot 0.0759278}$$

$$= \sqrt{0.0379639}$$

$$= 0.1948$$

But suppose that, hoping to help Cal, the 50 voters whose true ranking is Abe >Cal insincerely rank the candidates Eve >Abe >Cal on their ballots. Then a version of STV that does not transfer votes to already-elected candidates will first elect Abe, then eliminate Eve, then elect Cal (instead of Dee), and then elect Ben, thereby rewarding the 50 insincere voters. Table 39c shows the details.

To calculate the index of disproportionality for four factions when Abe, Cal and Dee win, we perform the following steps where S is the proportion of seats received and V is the proportion of votes received:

$$= \sqrt{\frac{1}{2} \sum_{factions} (S-V)^2}$$

$$= \sqrt{\frac{1}{2}\left(\left(\frac{1}{3} - \frac{155}{400}\right)^2 + \left(\frac{0}{3} - \frac{90}{400}\right)^2 + \left(\frac{1}{3} - \frac{80}{400}\right)^2 + \left(\frac{1}{3} - \frac{75}{400}\right)^2\right)}$$

$$= \sqrt{\frac{1}{2}\left((0.3333 - 0.3875)^2 + (0.0 - 0.225)^2 + (0.3333 - 0.2)^2 + (0.3333 - 0.1875)^2\right)}$$

$$= \sqrt{\frac{1}{2}\left(-0.54167^2 + -0.225^2 + 0.13333^2 + 0.1458^2\right)}$$

Table 39c: Outcome with Free Rider Voting and a Version of STV that Does Not Transfer Surplus to Already-Elected Candidates

	Stage				
	1	2	3	4	5
Exhausted Ballots	0	0	0	270	270
Quota	$400 \cdot \frac{1}{3+1}$ $= 100.0$	$400 \cdot \frac{1}{3+1}$ $= 100.0$	$400 \cdot \frac{1}{3+1}$ $= 100.0$	$400 \cdot \frac{1}{3+1}$ $= 100.0$	$400 \cdot \frac{1}{3+1}$ $= 100.0$
Votes for Abe	105	100.0	100.0	100.0	100.0
Votes for Ben	90	90	90	90	100.0
Votes for Cal	80	80	130	100.0	–
Votes for Dee	75	80.0	80.0	110.0	100.0
Votes for Eve	50	50	–	–	–
Votes not transferable	0	0	0	0	100.0
Total votes	400	400	400	400	400

Stage:

1: Because Abe has both more than a quota of votes and more votes than any other candidate, elect Abe; also, transfer Abe's surplus, i.e. $105 - 100.0 = 5.0$ votes, to the next choice(s) on the 105 ballots where Abe was first choice, i.e. to Dee, and set Abe's tally at the quota, that is, at 100.0.

2: Because no other candidate has more than a quota of votes and Eve has the fewest votes, eliminate Eve; also, transfer Eve's 50 votes, to the next not-yet elected and not-yet-eliminated choice(s) on the 50 ballots where Eve was top choice, i.e. to Cal.

3: Because Cal has both more than a quota of votes and more votes than any other candidate, elect Cal; also, transfer Cal's surplus, i.e. $130 - 100.0 = 30.0$ votes, to the next choice(s) on the 80 non-exhausted ballots where Cal was top choice, i.e. to Dee, and set Cal's tally at the quota, that is, at 100.0.

4: Because Dee has both more than a quota of votes and more votes than any other candidate, elect Dee and set Dee's tally at the quota, that is, at 100.0.

5: Crown Abe, Cal, and Dee.

$$= \sqrt{\frac{1}{2} \left(0.002934 + 0.050625 + 0.01777 + 0.02125764\right)}$$

$$= \sqrt{0.5 \cdot 0.0925943}$$

$$= \sqrt{0.046297}$$

$$= 0.2152$$

With Meek's method, in contrast, Abe, Dee, and Ben would, even with the free riding, be elected because, when Eve is eliminated, 50 fractions of a vote totaling 17.7 votes, instead of 50 whole votes, transfer from Abe to Cal. Table 39d shows the details.

To calculate the index of disproportionality for four factions when Abe, Cal and Dee win, we perform the following steps where S is the proportion of seats received and V is the proportion of votes received:

$$= \sqrt{\frac{1}{2} \sum_{factions} (S - V)^2}$$

$$= \sqrt{\frac{1}{2} \left(\left(\frac{1}{3} - \frac{155}{400}\right)^2 + \left(\frac{0}{3} - \frac{90}{400}\right)^2 + \left(\frac{1}{3} - \frac{80}{400}\right)^2 + \left(\frac{1}{3} - \frac{75}{400}\right)^2 \right)}$$

$$= \sqrt{\frac{1}{2} \left((0.3333 - 0.3875)^2 + (0.0 - 0.225)^2 + (0.3333 - 0.2)^2 + (0.3333 - 0.1875)^2 \right)}$$

$$= \sqrt{\frac{1}{2} \left(-0.54167^2 + -0.225^2 + 0.13333^2 + 0.1458^2 \right)}$$

$$= \sqrt{\frac{1}{2} \left(0.002934 + 0.050625 + 0.01777 + 0.02125764 \right)}$$

$$= \sqrt{0.5 \cdot 0.0925943}$$

$$= \sqrt{0.046297}$$

$$= 0.2152$$

Do not infer that Meek's method makes all kinds of tactical voting unrewarding. In 1992 and 2000, American political scientists John Duggan and Thomas Schwartz extended the Gibbard-Satterthwaite theorem to multi-winner elections, and the Duggan-Schwartz theorem applies to all multi-winner systems, including Meek's method.

The Duggan-Schwartz theorem says that, with any reasonable election system (that is, any system that can accommodate at least three candidates, will treat all candidates and voters equally, and will not automatically award victory to every voter's top choice), voters who know how others are voting may be able to obtain a more-preferred outcome by voting insincerely.[1]

---

[1] J. Duggan and T. Schwartz, "Strategic manipulability without resoluteness or shared beliefs: Gibbard-Satterthwaite generalized," Social Choice and Welfare 17: 85'93 (2000).

	Stage				
	1	2	3	4	5
Exhausted Ballots	0	0	0	270	270
Quota	$400 \cdot \frac{1}{3+1}$ $= 100.0$	$400 \cdot \frac{1}{3+1}$ $= 100.0$	$400 \cdot \frac{1}{3+1}$ $= 100.0$	$400 \cdot \frac{1}{3+1}$ $= 100.0$	$400 \cdot \frac{1}{3+1}$ $= 100.0$
Votes for Abe	105	100.0	100.0	100.0	100.0
Votes for Ben	90	90	90	102.3	100.0
Votes for Cal	80	80	97.7	97.7	–
Votes for Dee	75	80.0	112.3	100.0	100.0
Votes for Eve	50	50	–	–	–
Votes not transferable	0	0	0	0	100.0
Total votes	400	400	400	400	400

Index of disproportionality for four factions when Abe, Ben and Dee win = 0.1948.

Stage:

1: Because Abe has both more than a quota of votes and more votes than any other candidate, elect Abe; also, transfer Abe's surplus, i.e. $105 - 100.0 = 5.0$ votes, to the next choice(s) on the 105 ballots where Abe was first choice, i.e. to Dee, and set Abe's tally at the quota, that is, at 100.0.

2: Because no other candidate has more than a quota of votes and Eve has the fewest votes, eliminate Eve. Then transfer Eve's 50 votes to the next not-yet-eliminated choice(s) on the 50 ballots where Eve was top choice, i.e. to Abe. That raises Abe's tally without the 5-vote transfer from Abe to Dee to $105 + 50 = 155$. Now — since Abe was already elected, Cal was next choice on 50 ballots and Dee was next choice on 105 ballots — reverse the transfer of 5.0 votes from Abe to Dee and, instead, transfer $50 \cdot \left(1 - \frac{100}{155}\right) = 17.7$ votes from Abe to Cal and $105 \cdot \left(1 - \frac{100}{155}\right) = 37.3$ votes from Abe to Dee.

3: Because Dee has both at least a quota of votes and more votes than any other candidate, elect Dee; also, transfer Dee's surplus, i.e. $112.3 - 100.0 = 12.3$ votes, to the next not-yet-eliminated choice(s) on the ballots where Dee was top choice, i.e. to Ben, and set Dee's tally at the quota, that is, at 100.0.

4: Because Ben has both at least a quota of votes and more votes than any other candidate, elect Ben and set Ben's tally at the quota, that is, at 100.0.

5: Crown Abe, Ben, and Dee.

For example, even with Meek's method, insincerely ranking your real second choice first will initially give your real second choice a whole vote instead of a fraction transferred when your real first choice is elected and, as a result, may elect both instead of just one.

With a multi-winner system as well as a single-winner system, therefore, expect some tactical voting.

Bibliography

[1] Amendment XV Section 1, 42 U.S. Code Section 1973,. The Right of Citizens of the United States to Vote Shall Not Be Denied or Abridged.

[2] Douglas J Amy. *Real Choices/New Voices: How Proportional Representation Elections Could Revitalize American Democracy*. Columbia University Press, 2nd edition, 2002.

[3] Kenneth J Arrow. A Difficulty in the Concept of Social Welfare. *The Journal of Political Economy*, 58(4):328–346, 1950. JSTOR.

[4] Kenneth J Arrow. *Social Choice and Individual Values*. Wiley, New York, 1951.

[5] Kenneth J Arrow. *Social Choice and Individual Values*. Number 12. Yale University Press, 2nd edition, 1963.

[6] Kenneth J Arrow, Amartya Sen, and Kotaro Suzumura. *Handbook of Social Choice & Welfare*. Number 1. Elsevier, 2002.

[7] Australian Broadcasting Corporation. Australia Votes Federal Election, October 9, 2004. *ABC News Online*, 9 October 2004:Senate QLD, 2004. http://www.abc.net.au/elections/federal/2004/results/sendQLD.htm.

[8] Michel L Balinski and Rida Laraki. *Majority Judgment: Measuring, Ranking, and Electing*. MIT Press, 2010.

[9] Kathleen L Barber. *Proportional Representation and Election Reform in Ohio*. Ohio State University Press Columbus, OH, 1995.

[10] Duncan Black. On the Rationale of Group Decision-Making. *The Journal of Political Economy*, pages 23–34, 1948. JSTOR.

[11] Duncan Black, Robert Albert Newing, Iain McLean, Alistair McMillan, and Burt L Monroe. *The Theory of Committees and Elections*. Springer, page 69. 1958.

[12] Steven Brams. Mathematics and Democracy. *Princeton University Press*, 2(6):32, 2008.

[13] Steven J Brams and Peter C Fishburn. Approval Voting. *The American Political Science Review*, 72(3):831–847, 1978. JSTOR.

[14] Steven J Brams and Peter C Fishburn. Going From Theory to Practice: the Mixed Success of Approval Voting. *Social Choice and Welfare*, 25(2-3):457–474, 2005. Springer.

[15] Brown v. Smallwood. 130 Minn. 492, 153 N.W. 953, 1915.

[16] James W Bucklin. The Grand Junction Plan of City Government and Its Results. *Annals of the American Academy of Political and Social Science*, 38(3):87–102, 1911. JSTOR.

[17] California Elections Code, Section 14027.

[18] CIVS:Condorcet Internet Voting Service. http://civs.cs.cornell.edu/.

[19] Nathan Collins. Arrow's Theorem Proves No Voting System is Perfect. *MIT The Tech Online Edition*, 123(8):1–1, 2003. http://tech.mit.edu/V123/N8/8voting.8n.html.

[20] Clyde H Coombs. *A Theory of Data*. Wiley, 1964.

[21] Gary W Cox. *Making Votes Count: Strategic Coordination in the World's Electoral Systems*, volume 7. Cambridge Univ Press, 1997.

[22] Jean-Charles de Borda. Memoire sur les Elections au Scrutin, Historie de l'Academie Royale des Sciences. *Paris, France*, 1781.

[23] Marie Jean Antoine Nicolas de Caritat et al. *Essai sur L'application de L'analyse à la Probabilité des Décisions Rendues à la Pluralité des Voix*. L'Imprimerie Royale, Paris, 1785.

[24] Debian Constitution. http://www.debian.org/devel/constitution.

[25] Department of Justice. Cases Raising Claims Under Section 2 of the Voting Rights Act. http://www.justice.gov/crt/about/vot/litigation/recent_sec2.php#ncarolina.

[26] Victor d'Hondt. La Representation Proportionnelles des Partis par un Électeur. *Ghent (1882) Systéme Pratique et Raison de Représentation Proportionnelle. Brussels: Muquardt*, 1878.

[27] John Duggan and Thomas Schwartz. Strategic Manipulability Without Resoluteness or Shared Beliefs: Gibbard-Satterthwaite Generalized. *Social Choice and Welfare*, 17(1):85–93, 2000. Springer.

[28] Maurice Duverger. Duverger's Law: Forty Years Later. *Electoral Laws and their Political Consequences*, 1986. New York, Agathon Press.

[29] Eppley, Electoralwiki. Maximize Affirmed Majorities. wiki.electorama.com/wiki/Maximize_Affirmed_Majorities.

[30] Michael Gallagher. Proportionality, Disproportionality and Electoral Systems. *Electoral Studies*, 10(1):3–51, 1991. Elsevier.

[31] Michael Gallagher and Paul Mitchell. *The Politics of Electoral Systems*. Oxford University Press, 2005.

[32] Allan Gibbard. Manipulation of Voting Schemes: A General Result. *Econometrica: Journal of the Econometric Society*, 41(4):587–601, 1973. JSTOR.

[33] A Gierzynski, W Hamilton, and W Smith. Burlington Vermont 2009 IRV Mayor Election. *Range Voting Organization*, 2009. http://rangevoting.org/Burlington.html,2009.

[34] Gomez v. Hanford Joint Unified High School. Kings County Superior Court case no. 04C0294, (2004).

[35] Bernard Grofman and Scott L Feld. If You Like the Alternative Vote (aka the Instant Runoff), Then You Ought to Know About the Coombs Rule. *Electoral Studies*, 23(4):641–659, 2004. Elsevier.

[36] Bernard Grofman and Arend Lijphart. Electoral Laws and their Political Consequences. *Agathon Press*, 1986.

[37] I David Hill, BA Wichmann, and DR Woodall. Algorithm 123, Single Transferable Vote by Meek's Method. *Computer Journal UK*, 30(3):277–281, 1987.

[38] Edward V Huntington. The Mathematical Theory of the Apportionment of Representatives. *Proceedings of the National Academy of Sciences of the United States of America*, 7(4):123–127, 1921.

[39] Juho Laatu and Warren D. Smith. The rank-order votes in the 2009 burlington mayoral election, March 2009.

[40] A Lijphart, R Pintor, and Y Sone. The Limited Vote. *New York, Agathon Press*, page 168, 1986. B Grofman and A Lijphart's editions, Electoral Laws and their Political Consequences.

[41] Kenneth O May. A Set of Independent Necessary and Sufficient Conditions for Simple Majority Decision. *Econometrica: Journal of the Econometric Society*, 20(4):680–684, 1952. JSTOR.

[42] Brian L Meek. A New Approach to the Single Transferable Vote: Equality of Treatment of Voters and a Feedback Mechanism for Vote Counting. *Mathématiques et Sciences Humaines*, 25:13–23, 1969.

[43] Samuel Merrill III. A Comparison of Efficiency of Multi-Candidate Electoral Systems. *American Journal of Political Science*, 28:23–48, 1984. JSTOR.

[44] Robert G Moser and Ethan Scheiner. *Electoral Systems and Political Context: How the Effects of Rules Vary Across New and Established Democracies.* Cambridge University Press, 2012.

[45] Steven J Mulroy. Alternative Ways Out: A Remedial Road Map for the Use of Alternative Electoral Systems as Voting Rights Act Remedies. *NCL Rev.*, 77:1867, 1998. HeinOnline.

[46] Kenji Nakamura. The Vetoers in a Simple Game with Ordinal Preferences. *International Journal of Game Theory*, 8(1):55–61, 1979. Springer.

[47] New Zealand. Meek's Method STV Information. *Department of Internal Affairs*, 2014. http://www.dia.govt.nz/diawebsite.nsf/0/38f781eae0881449cc256c0f00152ea3?OpenDocument.

[48] Brian Olson. IRV Failure in the Real World, 2009. http://bolson.org/ bolson/2009/20090303_burlington.vt_mayor.html.

[49] Joseph T Ornstein and Robert Z Norman. Frequency of Monotonicity Failure Under Instant Runoff Voting: Estimates Based on a Spatial Model of Elections. *Public Choice*, pages 1–9, 2013. Springer.

[50] Range. Voting. scorevoting.net/WarrenSmithPages/homepage/rangevote.ps.

[51] Republic of Ireland. Guide to Ireland PR-STV Electoral System. *Franchise Section, Department of the Environment, Heritage and Local Government*, pages 1–8, 2011.

[52] Republic of Malta. Constitution: General Elections Act, Article 105.

[53] Rey v. Madera Unified School District. 138 Cal: Court of Appeal, 5th Appellate Dist. *Cal. App. 4th*, 203(No. F061532):1223, 2012.

[54] Andrew Reynolds, Ben Reilly, and Andrew Ellis. *Electoral System Design: the New International IDEA Handbook.* International Institute for Democracy and Electoral Assistance, Stockholm, 2005. pages 166-173.

[55] André Sainte-Laguë. La Représentation Proportionnelle et la Méthode des Moindres Carrés. In *Comptes Rendus Hebdomaires des Seances de l'Academie des Sciences*, volume 151, pages 377–78. Société Mathématique de France, 1910.

[56] Sanchez v. City of Modesto. 145 Cal: Court of Appeal, 5th Appellate Dist. *California Reporter 3d*, 51(No. F048277):821, 2006.

[57] Mark Allen Satterthwaite. Strategy-Proofness and Arrow's Conditions: Existence and Correspondence Theorems for Voting Procedures and Social Welfare Functions. *Journal of Economic Theory*, 10(2):187–217, 1975. Elsevier.

[58] Markus Schulze. A New Monotonic, Clone-Independent, Reversal Symmetric, and Condorcet-Consistent Single-Winner Election Method. *Social Choice and Welfare*, 36(2):267–303, 2011. Springer.

[59] Matthew Shugart and Martin P Wattenberg. *Mixed-Member Electoral Systems: The Best of Both Worlds?* Oxford University Press, 2001.

[60] Perry Smith. City Settles Lawsuit Voting Method to Change. *SCVTV MEDIA CENTER*, 2004/03/12, 2004. http://scvnews.com/2014/03/12/city-settles-lawsuit-voting-method-to-change/.

[61] T Nicolaus Tideman. Independence of Clones as a Criterion for Voting Rules. *Social Choice and Welfare*, 4(3):185–206, 1987. Springer.

[62] T Nicolaus Tideman. *Collective Decisions and Voting*. Ashgate Burlington, 2006. pages 165-244.

[63] Brian A Wichmann. Do the Differences Matter? *Voting Matters*, 14:4–5, 2001. http://www.votingmatters.org.uk/ISSUE14/P2.HTM.

[64] Robert Winters. Cambridge Municipal Elections. *Cambridge Civic Journal*, November, 2013. http://rwinters.com/elections/council2013.pdf.

[65] Douglas R Woodall. Monotonicity of Single-Seat Preferential Election Rules. *Discrete Applied Mathematics*, 77(1):81–98, 1997. Elsevier.

[66] Douglass R Woodall. Properties of Preferential Election Rules. *Voting Matters*, 3:8–15, 199, 1994.

[67] Thomas M Zavist and T Nicolaus Tideman. Complete Independence of Clones in the Ranked Pairs Rule. *Social Choice and Welfare*, 6(2):167–173, 1989. Springer.

Bibliography

Index

www.ingramcontent.com/pod-product-compliance
Lightning Source LLC
Chambersburg PA
CBHW081208280526
45787CB00006B/2371